T0300129

Harwood Fundamentals of Pure and Applied Economics

DESIGNING REGULATORY POLICY WITH LIMITED INFORMATION

FUNDAMENTALS OF PURE AND APPLIED ECONOMICS

EDITORS IN CHIEF

J. LESOURNE, Conservatoire National des Arts et Métiers, Paris, France
H. SONNENSCHEIN, University of Pennsylvania, Philadelphia, PA, USA

ADVISORY BOARD

K. ARROW, Stanford, CA, USA
W. BAUMOL, Princeton, NJ, USA
W. A. LEWIS, Princeton, NJ, USA
S. TSURU, Tokyo, Japan

ECONOMIC POLICY
In 3 Volumes

DESIGNING REGULATORY POLICY WITH LIMITED INFORMATION

DAVID BESANKO AND
DAVID E M SAPPINGTON

First published in 1987 by
Harwood Academic Publishers GmbH

Reprinted in 2001 by
Routledge
11 New Fetter Lane, London EC4P 4EE

Transferred to Digital Printing 2003

Routledge is an imprint of the Taylor & Francis Group

Printed and Bound in Great Britain

British Library Cataloguing in Publication Data
A CIP catalogue record for this book
is available from the British Library

Designing Regulatory Policy with Limited Information
ISBN 0-415-27463-X
Economic Policy: 3 Volumes
ISBN 0-415-26955-5
Harwood Fundamentals of Pure & Applied Economics
ISBN 0-415-26907-5

Designing Regulatory Policy with Limited Information

David Besanko
Indiana University, USA

and

David E. M. Sappington
Bell Communications Research, USA

A volume in the Government Ownership and Regulation of Economic Activity section

edited by

Elizabeth Bailey
Carnegie Mellon University, USA

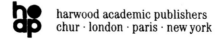

harwood academic publishers
chur · london · paris · new york

© 1987 by Harwood Academic Publishers GmbH
Poststrasse 22, 7000 Chur, Switzerland
All rights reserved

Harwood Academic Publishers

Post Office Box 197
London WC2E 9PX
England

58, rue Lhomond
75005 Paris
France

Post Office Box 786
Cooper Station
New York, NY 10276
United States of America

Library of Congress Cataloging-in-Publication Data

Besanko, David, 1955–
    Designing regulatory policy with limited information.

    (Fundamentals of pure and applied economics; vol. 20
    Government ownership and regulation of economic
    activity section, ISSN 0191–1708)
    Bibliography: p.
    Includes index.
    I. Trade regulation.   I. Sappington, David Edward
Michael.   II. Title.   III. Series: Fundamentals of pure and
applied economics, vol. 20.   IV. Series: Fundamentals of pure and
applied economics. Government ownership and regulation of
economic activity section.
K3842.B47   1987   350.82′6   87-277
ISBN 3-7186-0385-3

Contents

Introduction to the Series

Drawing on a personal network, an economist can still relatively easily stay well informed in the narrow field in which he works, but to keep up with the development of economics as a whole is a much more formidable challenge. Economists are confronted with difficulties associated with the rapid development of their discipline. There is a risk of "balkanisation" in economics, which may not be favorable to its development.

Fundamentals of Pure and Applied Economics has been created to meet this problem. The discipline of economics has been subdivided into sections (listed inside). These sections include short books, each surveying the state of the art in a given area.

Each book starts with the basic elements and goes as far as the most advanced results. Each should be useful to professors needing material for lectures, to graduate students looking for a global view of a particular subject, to professional economists wishing to keep up with the development of their science, and to researchers seeking convenient information on questions that incidentally appear in their work.

Each book is thus a presentation of the state of the art in a particular field rather than a step-by-step analysis of the development of the literature. Each is a high-level presentation but accessible to anyone with a solid background in economics, whether engaged in business, government, international organizations, teaching, or research in related fields.

Three aspects of *Fundamentals of Pure and Applied Economics* should be emphasized:

—First, the project covers the whole field of economics, not only theoretical or mathematical economics.

—Second, the project is open-ended and the number of books is not predetermined. If new interesting areas appear, they will generate additional books.

—Last, all the books making up each section will later be grouped to constitute one or several volumes of an Encyclopedia of Economics.

The editors of the sections are outstanding economists who have selected as authors for the series some of the finest specialists in the world.

J. Lesourne   *H. Sonnenschein*

Designing Regulatory Policy with Limited Information

DAVID BESANKO
Department of Business Economics and Public Policy, Indiana University

DAVID E. M. SAPPINGTON
Economics Research Group, Bell Communications Research, Inc.

1. INTRODUCTION

The purpose of this monograph is to review and interpret the literature that examines the design of regulatory policy when the regulator's knowledge of the relevant environment is limited. For the most part, we are concerned with natural monopoly settings. Thus, a regulator is appointed to exercise the discipline on the monopoly firm that competition might otherwise provide. If the regulator were perfectly informed about demand and cost conditions in the industry, his task would be relatively straightforward. The optimal regulatory policy when the regulator is perfectly informed about the environment in which the firm operates is well documented in the literature. (See, for example, [13] and [61].) In practice, however, regulators are not likely to be perfectly informed about technological and demand conditions in the industries they oversee. Thus, a question arises as to whether optimal regulatory policy differs significantly when the regulator's knowledge is limited. It turns out that this is the case, which is why we believe this monograph discusses an important line of research.

Our task is facilitated by the fact that this is a relatively recent area of formal research. Nevertheless, it is inevitable that we have

The first author gratefully acknowledges the support of the National Science Foundation through Grant No. SES-8408335. The views expressed in this paper are not necessarily those of Bell Communications Research, Inc. We are grateful to Martin Perry for his helpful suggestions.

1

inadvertently overlooked some important contributions to the field. We apologize in advance for *our* limited information. We also wish to point out three complementary reviews of the literature . . . those of Baron [6], Caillaud *et al.* [20] and Sappington and Stiglitz [78].

Our treatment of the literature is varied. In early sections, we carefully specify the model under consideration and state formally the major conclusions drawn from the model. We also outline the proofs of these conclusions to provide a feel for the analytic techniques commonly employed in this literature. In later sections our review becomes less rigorous and more intuitive. We summarize and explain the major findings, and refer the interested reader to the appropriate source for a more detailed derivation of the conclusions.

Our style is to offer little criticism of particular works as we proceed through the review. We largely reserve general criticism for the concluding section, where we outline directions in which we feel research should proceed.

Our discussion begins in Section 2 with a very brief historical review and statement of the class of problems on which our discussion is focused. The solution to non-repeated adverse selection problems is the subject of Section 3. These problems assume that the regulated monopolist is endowed with private technological information and/or capabilities from the outset. The regulator's task is to set prices and taxes to control the rents the firm commands from its superior knowledge. The prices implemented by the regulator who is imperfectly informed about the firm's environment will generally differ from those that are optimal in the presence of perfect information. The nature of the differences are explored in some detail. The differences are re-examined in Section 4 where the regulator is presumed to have an additional policy instrument at his disposal. In particular, the regulator is able to purchase an imperfect observation (audit) of the firm's costs of production. The use of this costly audit instrument, as well as its effect on the use of other instruments, is examined in some detail.

In Section 5, the related problem of moral hazard is considered. Here, even though realized production costs may be costlessly observed by the regulator, the effort expended by the firm aimed at cost reduction is not observable. Thus, the regulator cannot be certain whether high cost realizations are due to unfavorable technological conditions or to lack of diligent effort by the firm. The regulator's task in this setting is to motivate cost reduction. Some thoughts on the interplay between moral hazard and adverse selection problems are also recorded in this section.

Repeated interactions between regulator and firm are explored in Section 6. With repeated play, the regulator is afforded multiple observations of the firm's performance, and is often better able to limit the firm's rents as a consequence. To a large extent, the value of repeated observations to the regulator depends upon his ability to make binding commitments concerning how he will employ information gleaned from present performance to structure future rewards for the firm. This central issue of intertemporal commitment ability is examined in Section 7.

In Section 8, we consider the effects of introducing potential and actual competition into the regulatory process. The optimal structuring of franchise bidding and entry policy is considered. We also examine the manner in which the performance of local monopolies across related jurisdictions is optimally compared. Finally, in Section 9, we attempt to outline the directions in which research in this important area is proceeding.

2. BACKGROUND: HISTORY AND RELATED LITERATURE

Formal models of regulation have a long history. Economists have been concerned for some time with how to set prices in regulated industries. The work of Dupuit [26] and Hotelling [43] demonstrated the value of equating price and marginal cost. Ramsey [66] and Baumol and Bradford [13] identified optimal "second-best" prices: prices that maximize welfare while ensuring non-negative profit for a multiproduct monopolist who produces with increasing returns to scale. Significant attention has also been given to such issues as optimal peak-load prices (see, for example, [83], [90], and [61]); fair rate of return regulation (see, for example, [2] and [14]); sustainable prices (e.g., [62]); and subsidy-free prices (e.g., [28]).

A distinguishing feature of most of these analyses was the assumption of perfect information. Both the regulator and the firm were presumed to have completely accurate and comprehensive information about cost and demand conditions in the industry.

It was not until the 1970s that models of pricing under conditions of imperfect knowledge began to emerge in some force. One such class of models that influenced subsequent formal models of regulation investigated the nature of optimal non-linear price schedules when the monopolist was uncertain about the preferences of his customers. (See, for example, [70], [81], and [33].) This literature developed in tandem with the optimal tax literature (see, for example, [58]), principal-agent literature (e.g., [73], [38], [39], [41], and [80]) and the sharecropping literature (e.g., [84]). All of the bodies of work addressed related issues of private information and incentives, and had a strong influence on the literature that is reviewed in this monograph.

There are a great variety of ways in which imperfect information impinges on the regulatory setting. Aside from consumer preferences being unknown, aspects of the current production technology may be unknown to the regulator and/or the firm. The likely consequences of research and development may also be uncertain. And certain activities (such as effort exerted by the firm's managers) may not be perfectly observed by all parties. All of these possibilities will be considered below, though the focus here (as in the literature) is on the incentive problem that arises when the firm has private technological information that is not shared by the regulator. This adverse selection problem is the focus of Section 3.

3. ADVERSE SELECTION

Perhaps the most basic problem facing the regulator is the "one-shot" adverse selection problem. An adverse selection problem is said to arise when relevant characteristics of one party to a relationship (e.g., the regulated firm) cannot be observed by another party (e.g., the regulator). Thus, an example of our focus here is when the firm has better information about its productive capabilities than does the regulator from the onset of their non-repeated relationship. We describe the solution to the one-shot adverse selection problem in this section in a series of steps. First, we solve the simplest adverse selection problem, in which the firm's private cost information is the realization of a binary random variable. The regulator's policy instruments are also restricted in this simple setting. In particular, the regulator is presumed able to dictate only a uniform price and a subsidy. Second, we demonstrate how the basic insights of the binary model extend to the setting where the random cost parameter has a continuous distribution. Third, we examine how the regulator will optimally employ additional information that may be at his disposal. In particular, when the firm's choice of capital is observable, we explore how the firm is optimally compensated as a function of the amount of capital it installs. This leads us to reconsider the Averch–Johnson [2] model of rate-of-return regulation in a setting where adverse selection complicates the regulator's task.

3.1. Binary uncertainty

The simplest (Bayesian) model of adverse selection is that in which there is a single cost parameter that is known to the firm but not to the regulator. Moreover, the parameter, c, can take on only one of two possible values (i.e., $c \in \{c_L, c_H\}$ with $c_H > c_L$). The regulator's beliefs about the actual realization of c are given by $\phi_i > 0$, which is the probability that $c = c_i$. Of course, $\phi_L = \phi_H = 1$.

The higher realization of the cost parameter is presumed to capture uniformly higher production costs for the firm. Letting $C(x, c)$ represent the firm's total cost of producing output level x when the realized cost parameter is c, the following assumptions are introduced. Alphabetic subscripts (here and throughout) will denote partial derivatives.

Assumption 3.1 $C(x, c) > 0$, $\forall x > 0$.

Assumption 3.2 $C_x(x, c) > 0$, $\forall x > 0$.

Assumption 3.3 $C(x, c_H) > C(x, c_L)$, $\forall x > 0$.

Assumption 3.4 $C_x(x, c_H) > C_x(x, c_L)$, $\forall x > 0$.

Assumptions 3.1 and 3.2 simply state that total and marginal costs of production are positive. These assumptions are maintained throughout our entire discussion. Assumptions 3.3 and 3.4 imply that a higher realization of c corresponds to higher total and marginal production costs. The importance of Assumption 3.4, known as the "single crossing" property, is explained below.

The regulator's presumed objective is to maximize a weighted average of consumers' surplus, S, and profit of the regulated firm. The weights on consumers' surplus and profit will be taken to be β and $1 - \beta$, respectively, with $\beta \in (1/2, 1]$. Thus, the regulator "cares more" about consumers' surplus than profit. Absent this restriction, the incentive problem becomes trivial, as the regulator will optimally delegate all decision-making to the firm, knowing that it will employ its superior information to maximize its profit.

Though the regulator does not know the actual realization of c at the time he must design an incentive scheme for the firm, he is presumed to know both the demand function $X(p)$ for the firm's output (where p represents price) and the form of the firm's cost function. The regulator is also assumed to know the minimum level of profit, $\bar{\pi}$, required to induce the firm to operate. Thus, all uncertainty is captured in the single technological parameter, c. Note that it is presumed prohibitively costly for the regulator to observe total production costs or any related measure of costs. (This assumption is modified in Section 4.)

The regulator is also presumed able to precommit himself to the terms of any incentive scheme. In other words, once the regulator has announced how the firm will be compensated for its output, he cannot renege on the promised payment. (This important assumption is re-examined in Section 7.)

The regulator's strategy in this setting is the following. The firm is offered a choice between two prices, p_L and p_H, and associated taxes, T_L and T_H. The magnitudes of these variables are designed so that the firm will set price p_i, produce $X(p_i)$, and pay tax T_i when the realized cost parameter is c_i.[1] For simplicity, the regulator is presumed able to subsidize the firm with funds raised via non-distortionary taxes. Thus $T_i < 0$ is feasible, and the only cost of a subsidy to the firm is the concomitant direct reduction in consumers' surplus. The optimal structure of prices and taxes is determined by solving the following binary representation of the regulator's problem [RP-B].

---

[1] Thus, we presume the firm serves all demand at the regulated price. It is not difficult to show that the regulator will never optimally induce the firm to produce less output than is demanded at the regulated price. Similarly, the regulator will never find it advantageous to have the firm produce more output than is sold to customers.

Maximize $\displaystyle\sum_{i=L}^{H} \phi_i\{\beta[S(p_i) + T_i] + [1 - \beta]\pi(p_i, T_i; c_i)\}$,

subject to:

$$\pi(p_i, T_i; c_i) \geq \bar{\pi} \qquad\qquad i \in \{L, H\}. \qquad (3.1)$$

$$\pi(p_i, T_i; c_i) \geq \pi(p_j, T_j; c_i) \qquad i, j \in \{L, H\}, \qquad (3.2)$$

where

$$\pi(p_j, T_j; c_i) = p_j X(p_j) - C(X(p_j), c_i) - T_j.$$

The individual rationality constraints (3.1) guarantee the firm a level of profit that does not fall short of its reservation level. Thus, whatever its private technological information, the firm will agree to the terms of the regulatory contract. The self-selection constraints (3.2) identify $\{p_i, T_i\}$ as the price-tax combination that the firm will select when $c = c_i$.[2]

If the regulator shared the firm's private technological information, he would implement what is termed the first-best solution to [RP-B].

DEFINITION 3.1 The first-best solution to [RP-B] is that price and tax such that $\forall i \in \{L, H\}$

i) $\pi(p_i, T_i; c_i) = \bar{\pi}$, and

ii) $p_i = C_x(x_i, c_i)$,

where $x_i = X(p_i)$.

Thus, the most preferred outcome for the regulator holds the firm to its reservation profit level and ensures that the total surplus is as large as possible (via implementing marginal-cost prices) for both cost realizations.[3] We will denote the first-best price and output levels for $c = c_i$ as p_i^* and $X(p_i^*) = x_i^*$, respectively.

Before proceeding it is important to emphasize that in our

---

[2] Throughout, it is assumed that when indifferent among alternatives, the firm will choose according to the regulator's preferences. This assumption avoids an uninteresting open set problem.

[3] If, on the other hand, subsidies were prohibitively costly, the relevant first-best benchmark would be Ramsey prices rather than marginal cost prices. (See Ramsey [66] and Baumol and Bradford [13].)

analysis the firm is assumed to have acquired its private information before the regulatory policy is formulated. That is why in (3.1) there is an individual rationality constraint for each possible realization of the cost parameter. If, as an alternative, the regulatory policy were formulated before the firm received its private information, the constraints in (3.1) would be replaced by a constraint that required expected profits to exceed the reservation level $\bar{\pi}$. In this case Baron [3] has shown that if the regulator and the firm have symmetric expectations about production costs, the regulator can implement marginal cost pricing and extract all expected rents from the firm. With identical beliefs, the firm and the regulator would agree on the maximum expected level of surplus that could be generated. The risk-neutral firm could then be given title to the realized surplus in return for an initial lump-sum payment equal to the difference between the expected surplus and $\bar{\pi}$. After subsequently observing actual production costs the firm would act to maximize total surplus (by setting price equal to marginal cost). The initial lump-sum payment (which can be interpreted as a franchise fee) would eliminate all anticipated rents for the firm.[4]

Of primary concern here is how the initial information asymmetry between regulator and firm causes the optimal regulatory policy to deviate from the first-best solution to [RP-B]. The critical differences are recorded in Proposition 3.1 and Corollaries 3.1–3.3.

PROPOSITION 3.1   *Under Assumptions* 3.1–3.4, *the solution to* [RP-B] *has the following features:*

   i) $\pi(p_H, T_H; c_H) = \bar{\pi}$.

   ii) $\pi(p_L, T_L; c_L) = \pi(p_H, T_H; c_L)$.

   iii) $p_L = C_x(x_L, c_L)$.

   iv) $p_H = C_x(x_H, c_H) + \phi_L[2\beta - 1][\phi_H\beta]^{-1}$
       $\times [C_x(x_H, c_H) - C_x(x_H, c_L)]$.

---

[4] This incentive scheme, which effectively decentralizes all decision-making to the firm, has been discussed in the principal-agent literature by Harris and Raviv [38], Holmstrom [41], and Shavell [80]. Riordan [67] derives a related conclusion in a model where demand (rather than cost) information is observed privately by the firm.

Proof. Let θ_i and θ_{ij} be the Lagrange multipliers associated with constraints (3.1) and (3.2), respectively. Then, the necessary conditions for a solution to [RP-B] include:

$$\phi_i[2\beta - 1] - [\theta_i + \theta_{ij}] + \theta_{ji} = 0, \qquad j \neq i, \qquad i, j \in \{L, H\}, \quad (3.3)$$

$$\beta\phi_i S'(p_i) + [(1 - \beta)\phi_i + \theta_i + \theta_{ij}]\pi_p(p_i, T_i; c_i)$$
$$- \theta_{ji}\pi_p(p_i, T_i; c_j) = 0, \qquad j \neq i, \qquad i, j \in \{L, H\}, \quad (3.4)$$

where $S'(p_i) = -X(p_i)$ represents the derivative of consumers' surplus with respect to price. (Here and throughout, derivatives of a function of a single variable are denoted by "primes.") Using (3.3), (3.4) can be rewritten as:

$$p_i = C_x(x_i, c_i) + \theta_{ji}[\beta\phi_i]^{-1}[C_x(x_i, c_i) - C_x(x_i, c_j)],$$
$$j \neq i, \qquad i, j \in \{L, H\}. \quad (3.5)$$

If $X(p_H) > 0$, it follows immediately from (3.1) and (3.2) that $\theta_L = 0$. Then, presuming $\theta_{HL} = 0$, it follows from (3.3) that $\theta_{LH} = \phi_L[2\beta - 1] > 0$, and $\theta_H = 2\beta - 1 > 0$. Thus, conditions (i) and (ii) of the proposition are proved, and conditions (iii) and (iv) follow from (3.5). Finally, to confirm that $\theta_{HL} = 0$, note that since

$$\pi(p_L, T_L; c_H) = p_L x_L - C(x_L, c_H) - T_L$$
$$= \pi(p_L, T_L; c_L) + C(x_L, c_L) - C(x_L, c_H),$$
$$= \pi(p_H, T_H; c_L) + C(x_L, c_L) - C(x_L, c_H).$$

it follows that

$$\pi(p_H, T_H; c_H) - \pi(p_L, T_L; c_H) = C(x_L, c_H) - C(x_L, c_L)$$
$$- [C(x_H, c_H) - C(x_H, c_L)] > 0,$$

since $x_L > x_H$, and Assumption 3.4 implies that marginal costs increase with c.

COROLLARY 3.1 *In the solution to* [RP-B], *the firm earns no rents when the higher cost parameter is realized. Rents will be strictly positive, though, when low costs are realized, provided* $x_H > 0$.

COROLLARY 3.2 *In the solution to* [RP-B], $p_H > p_H^*$ *and* $p_L = p_L^*$.

COROLLARY 3.3 *In the solution to* [RP-B], x_H *is smaller the smaller is* ϕ_H.

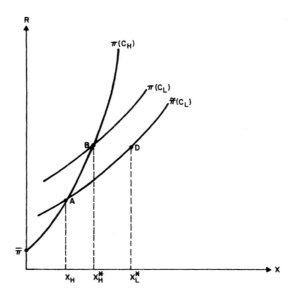

FIGURE 3.1   The solution to [RP-B], {A, D}.

To ensure that the firm will produce $(x_H > 0)$ when realized production costs are high, the regulator must compensate the firm according to the cost function $C(x_H, c_H)$. In terms of Figure 3.1, the total payment to the firm, $R = pX(p) - T$, must be sufficient to keep it on or above (i.e., to the northwest of) the iso-profit curve labelled $\pi(c_H)$. This locus represents combinations of payments and output levels that provide the same profit to the firm with cost parameter c_H as a payment of $\bar{\pi}$ for zero output. Note that the firm's profit in Figure 3.1 increases with movements in a northwesterly direction. If the firm's cost parameter were known to be c_H, the regulator would instruct the firm to expand output to the first-best level, x_H^*, where the marginal cost and benefit of incremental output are equated. Point B in Figure 3.1 represents this outcome.

Note, however, that if $c = c_L$, the firm earns strictly positive rents from the production-compensation pair represented by point B. This is evident from the fact that the $\pi(c_L)$ iso-profit curve (the relevant iso-profit locus when $c = c_L$) that passes through point B is flatter than $\pi(c_H)$, and thus hits the vertical axis above $\bar{\pi}$. The flatter slope reflects the lower production costs when c_L is realized.

To induce the firm with cost parameter c_L to accept any output-compensation pair other than, say, that represented by point B, the other pair must lie to the northwest of the $\pi(c_L)$ iso-profit locus. Note that movements downward and to the left along the $\pi(c_H)$ locus keep the profit of the firm constant when $c = c_H$, but reduce the firm's profit when $c = c_L$. This is because a reduction in output reduces the difference in total production costs according to the realization of c, and thereby reduces the rents the firm can secure when $c = c_L$ by producing the output level that the regulator will have the firm produce when costs are high (c_H). Thus, by inducing the firm to produce output x_H (at point A) rather than x_H^* (at point B) when $c = c_H$, the rents that accrue to the firm when $c = c_H$. If ϕ_H is sufficiently low, x_H may be established at a level below that which a monopolist with costs $C(x, c_H)$ would produce. always some neighborhood around x_H^* in which the cost is outweighed by the benefits of reduced payments to the firm when $c = c_L$.[5]

The magnitude of the optimal reduction in output below x_H^* depends, in part, upon the regulator's beliefs about the firm's costs. The more certain is the regulator that $c = c_L$, the more important it is to limit the rents that the firm will command when its costs are low, and therefore the smaller will be the induced output when $c = c_H$. If ϕ_H is sufficiently low, x_H may be established at a level below that which a monopolist with costs $C(x, c_H)$ would produce. In fact, it is possible that the regulator will not have the firm produce at all if $c = c_H$, even though the social gains from production outweigh the associated production costs.[6]

In all cases, the firm will produce the first-best level of output when $c = c_L$. This is accomplished by compensating the firm for

---

[5] Technically, the first order effect on total surplus of deviations from the first-best output level is zero. This observation follows from the fact that

$$\partial\{CS(x) + \pi(x; c_i)\}/\partial x|_{x=x_i} = p_i - C_x(x_i, c_i) = 0.$$

[6] This possibility is more likely the smaller is ϕ_H and the larger is $C(x, c_H) - C(x, c_L)$, *ceteris paribus*. Whether the firm will ever be shut down altogether also depends upon the behavior of the consumers' surplus function in the neighborhood of $x = 0$. See [12] for additional insight on this matter.

output in excess of x_H according to costs $C(x, c_L)$. This rate of compensation (represented by movement along iso-profit curve $\bar{\pi}(c_L)$ in Figure 3.1) ensures that the firm will produce the higher level of output if and only if $c = c_L$. Assumption 3.4 $(C_x(x, c_H) > C_x(x, c_L))$ implies that costs rise more rapidly with output under c_H than under c_L. Thus, iso-profit loci, $\bar{\pi}(c_L)$ and $\pi(c_H)$ for example, cross only once, ensuring that the firm will strictly prefer point A to any other point further to the right along $\bar{\pi}(c_L)$ when $c = c_H$. Consequently, the regulator's only concern in setting x_L is to generate the greatest possible total surplus when $c = c_L$. By definition, this is accomplished by setting $x_L = x_L^*$. The subsidy awarded the firm for producing x_L leaves the firm indifferent between producing x_L and x_H when $c = c_L$. Thus, in Figure 3.1, the output-compensation pair that will be selected by the firm when $c = c_L$ is at point D, on the $\bar{\pi}(c_L)$ iso-profit locus through point A.

3.2. The continuous analysis

Restricting the support of the random variable to be binary facilitates an understanding of the basic logic that underlies the optimal regulatory policy. It is important, however, to determine how the essential conclusions (in Proposition 3.1 and Corollaries 3.1–3.3) are modified when more general representations of the crucial information asymmetry are admitted. To this end, we now consider a model in which the firm's cost parameter, c, can take on any one of a continuum of values in an arbitrary closed interval, denoted $[c^-, c^+]$. The continuous model of regulatory policy with adverse selection was first analyzed by Baron and Myerson [12], and our discussion in this section is based largely on their important contribution.

In this continuous analysis we represent the regulator's prior beliefs about c by a distribution function $F:[c^-, c^+] \rightarrow [0, 1]$. The associated density function is represented by $f(c) \equiv F'(c)$. We assume:

Assumption 3.5 f is continuously differentiable with strictly positive support on $[c^-, c^+]$.

In addition, we assume:

Assumption 3.6 $F(c)[f(c)]^{-1}$ is a non-decreasing function of c.

Assumption 3.6 is a regularity condition on beliefs that is common in this literature. Its importance is discussed in footnote 8 below. Assumption 3.6 is satisfied by a number of well-known distribution functions including the uniform, exponential, and normal.

In the continuous analysis, some assumptions on the cost function in addition to Assumptions 3.1 and 3.2 are helpful. These are:

Assumption 3.7 $C_c > 0$ $\forall\, x, c.$

Assumption 3.8 $C_{xc} > 0$ $\forall\, x, c.$

Assumption 3.9 $C_{xx} \geq 0$ $\forall\, x, c.$

Assumption 3.10 $C_{xxc} \geq 0$ $\forall\, x, c.$

Assumption 3.11 $C_{xcc} \geq 0$ $\forall\, x, c.$

Assumptions 3.7 and 3.8 are analogous to 3.3 and 3.4 in the binary case. Assumption 3.9 says that marginal cost increases as output increases, and Assumption 3.10 states that the rate of increase is itself an increasing function of c. Assumption 3.11 indicates that the rate at which marginal cost increases with c is itself increasing in c. Assumptions 3.9 and 3.10 are made to ensure that the relevant second-order conditions are satisfied. The role of Assumption 3.11 is similar to that of 3.8 and will be discussed below. It is apparent that these assumptions are satisfied by a linear cost function $C(x, c) = cx + K$. They are also satisfied by any cost function of the form $c\Gamma(x)$ where Γ is a convex function.[7]

To represent the regulator's problem formally in this setting, an approach analogous to that employed in the binary setting is adopted. Without loss of generality, the regulator can be modeled as offering the firm a choice of a particular price-tax pair from a judiciously designed schedule of price and tax combinations, $\{p(c), T(c)\}$. In effect, the pricing decision is delegated completely to the firm, but each possible price level is associated with a specific tax that the firm must pay. Provided that the schedule, $\{p(c), T(c)\}$, is structured to satisfy the relevant individual rationality and self-selection constraints, it is possible to index the price and associated tax by the cost parameter of the firm. Thus, for example, $p(\hat{c})$ represents the equilibrium price charged by a firm

---

[7] Baron and Myerson's [12] original analysis of this problem used the linear specification.

with cost parameter $\hat{c}$, and $T(\hat{c})$ represents the tax levied on the firm when price $p(\hat{c})$ is charged.

Formally, with a continuum of possible costs, the regulator's problem is to choose price and tax schedules, $p(c)$ and $T(c)$, to solve the following problem, which we label [RP-C].

Maximize $\displaystyle\int_{c^-}^{\bar{c}} \{\beta[S(p(c)) + T(c)] + [1 - \beta][\pi(p(c),$
$$T(c); c) - \bar{\pi}]\}f(c)\, dc$$

subject to:

$$\pi(p(c), T(c); c) \geq \bar{\pi} \qquad \forall\, c \in [c^-, c^+], \tag{3.6}$$

$$\pi(p(c), T(c); c) \geq \pi(p(\hat{c}), T(\hat{c}); c) \qquad \forall c, \hat{c} \in [c^-, c^+], \tag{3.7}$$

and

$$c^- \leq \bar{c} \leq c^+. \tag{3.8}$$

The variable $\bar{c}$ represents the highest cost at which production will take place. Constraint (3.6) is the individual rationality constraint analogous to (3.1) in the binary model, and constraint (3.7) is the self-selection constraint analogous to (3.2) in the binary model.

To serve as a benchmark for the solution to [RP-C], the first-best solution to the regulator's problem is defined.

DEFINITION 3.2 The first-best solution to [RP-C] is a pair of functions $\{p^*(c), T^*(c)\}$ and an upper limit $\bar{c}^*$ such that $\forall\, c$:

   i) $p^*(c) = C_x(X(p^*(c)), c)$.
   ii) $\pi(p^*(c), T^*(c); c) = \bar{\pi}$.
   iii) $\bar{c}^* = \min\{c^+, \tilde{c}^*\}$, where $\tilde{c}^*$ is defined by:

$$S(p^*(\tilde{c}^*)) + p^*(\tilde{c}^*)X(p^*(\tilde{c}^*)) - C(X(p^*(\tilde{c}^*)), \tilde{c}^*) - \bar{\pi} = 0.$$

Thus, as in the binary case, the first-best solution involves a price equal to marginal cost and a tax that extracts all rents from the firm. Furthermore, production always occurs as long as the expected total surplus exceeds total production costs.

The analysis of [RP-C] can be simplified by the following lemma, whose proof is in the Appendix to Section 3.

LEMMA 3.1 *Any solution to* [RP-C] *is also a solution to the following problem, and vice versa. Thus the two problems are equivalent:*

Maximize $\displaystyle\int_{c^-}^{\bar{c}} \{V(x(c)) - C(x(c), c) - H(c)C_c(x(c), c) - \bar{\pi}\}f(c)\,dc$ (3.9)

subject to:

$$c^- \leq \bar{c} \leq c^+, \tag{3.8}$$

$$T(c) = P(x(c))x(c) - C(x(c), c) - \int_c^{\bar{c}} C_c(x(t), t)\,dt - \bar{\pi}, \tag{3.10}$$

$$p(c) = P(x(c)), \tag{3.11}$$

and

$$x(c) = X(p(c)) \text{ is non-increasing}, \tag{3.12}$$

where $P(x)$ denotes the inverse demand function, $V(x) = \int_0^x P(t)\,dt$, and $H(c) \equiv [2\beta - 1]\beta^{-1}F(c)[f(c)]^{-1} \geq 0$.

The transformed problem stated in Lemma 3.1 facilitates characterization of the optimal regulatory policy. The optimal output schedule, $x(c)$, can be found by maximizing the integrand in (3.9). The optimal tax and price schedules can then be determined from (3.10) and (3.11), respectively. The next proposition summarizes the results of this procedure.

PROPOSITION 3.2 *Under Assumptions 3.1, 3.2, and 3.5–3.11, the solution to [RP-C] has the following features:*

$$P(x(c)) = C_x(x(c), c) + H(c)C_{xc}(x(c), c), \tag{3.13}$$

and

$$\bar{c} = \min(c^+, \tilde{c}), \quad \text{where } \tilde{c} \text{ is defined by:}$$
$$V(x(\tilde{c})) - C(x(\tilde{c}), \tilde{c}) - H(\tilde{c})C_c(x(\tilde{c}), \tilde{c}) - \bar{\pi} = 0. \tag{3.14}$$

Proof. Pointwise maximization of (3.9) with respect to x yields (3.13). Assumptions 3.9 and 3.10 can be shown to imply that the integrand is a strictly concave function of x, so (3.13) is a necessary and sufficient condition for pointwise maximization of (3.9). To verify that the monotonicity constraint (3.12) is satisfied, differentiate each side of (3.13) with respect to c, and rearrange terms to obtain

$$x'(c) = [(1 + H')C_{xc} + HC_{xcc}][P' - C_{xx} - HC_{xxc}]^{-1}.$$

Assumptions 3.6 and 3.8–3.11 imply that $x'(c) > 0$.

Differentiating the integral with respect to $\bar{c}$ leads to (3.14).[8]

---

[8] In the proof of Proposition 3.2, the monotonicity of $F(c)[f(c)]^{-1}$ along with Assumptions 3.8 and 3.11 played an important role in ensuring that the monotonicity constraint (3.12) is satisfied. If any of these assumptions is dropped, the $x(c)$ that maximizes the integrand in (3.9) may violate (3.12). This possibility is depicted in Figure F.1. In this case the optimal solution $x(c)$ can be found using a technique developed by Baron and Myerson [12] and Guesnerie and Laffont [36]. The way this technique would work in the case of the $x(c)$ depicted in Figure F.1 is to find values $\bar{x}$, c_1, and c_2 such that

$$x(c_1) = \bar{x},$$
$$x(c_2) = \bar{x},$$

and

$$P(\bar{x}) = \int_{c_1}^{c_2} \{C_x(\bar{x}, c) + H(c)C_{xc}(\bar{x}, c)\}f(c)\, dc.$$

Thus, the $x(c)$ function would be "convexified" over an interval $[c_1, c_2]$ in such a way that price $P(\bar{x})$ equals the expected value of marginal cost plus the deviation term. Thus, over the interval $[c_1, c_2]$ the solution to [RP-B] exhibits 'pooling' of types, in that the firm will produce the same level of output for all these realizations of c.

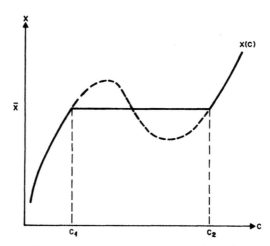

FIGURE F.1   Pooling solution to [RP-C].

At the solution to [RP-C], there are two sources of inefficiency relative to the first-best solution. First, as equation (3.13) reveals, price exceeds marginal cost (since $H(c) \geq 0$ and $C_{xc}(\cdot) > 0$ by Assumption 3.8). Second, since $\bar{c} \leq \bar{c}^*$, equation (3.14) indicates that firms with high costs are more likely to be shut down completely.

Some intuition regarding the optimal regulatory policy is provided in the corollaries that follow.

COROLLARY 3.4 i) *Under the solution to* [RP-C] *the realized profit for a firm with cost parameter* c, $\pi(c)$, *is given by:*

$$\pi(c) = \int_c^{\bar{c}} C_c(x(t), t)\, dt + \bar{\pi}; \qquad (3.15)$$

ii) *This profit is decreasing in* c (*i.e.,* $\pi'(c) < 0$), *and is equal to the reservation profit when* $c = \bar{c}$ (*i.e.,* $\pi(\bar{c}) = \bar{\pi}$).

The firm earns rents because it possesses private information. With actual costs unobservable, and the regulator's policy instruments quite limited, the firm must be "bribed" to reveal low cost realizations. The lower are actual costs, the greater the rents that must be awarded the firm. Expression (3.15) implies that these rents decrease at the rate at which total costs increase with c, i.e., at the rate C_c. This is the case because the potential gain to a firm with cost parameter $c_0 - \tau$ from choosing the price and tax pair designed for a firm with cost parameter c_0 (i.e., from "exaggerating costs") is approximately equal to $\tau C_c(x(c_0), c_0)$, reflecting the firm's cost advantage. Thus, to induce truthful cost reporting, the (approximate) difference in rents, $\tau \pi'(c)$, must just offset this potential benefit.

COROLLARY 3.5 *At the solution to* [RP-C], *the firm is induced to charge a price in excess of marginal cost* $\forall c > c^-$. *Price and marginal cost are equal only when* $c = c^-$.

To interpret Corollary 3.5, suppose the regulator chose to induce the first-best output $x^*(c_1)$ for a firm with cost parameter $c = c_1$ where $c_1 > c^-$. Because $x^*(c_1)$ is the level of output that maximizes social welfare when $c = c_1$, a slight downward deviation of output below $x^*(c_1)$ has no effect on social welfare when $c = c_1$. (Recall footnote 5.) However, because $C_{xc} > 0$, the output reduction lowers the profit that would be earned by a firm whose costs are less than c_1 under the output-tax pair $(x(c_1), T(c_1))$. Consequently, by decreasing output the regulator can increase the taxes levied on firms with costs below c_1 without inducing them to exaggerate their costs. The key point is that by distorting output downward, the regulator trades off welfare losses when $c = c_1$ (due to the output reduction) with increases in taxes that can be collected when $c < c_1$. The rate at which taxes decrease as a function of increases in output is C_{xc}. The direct losses from output reductions are incurred with probability $f(c_1)$. The gains from additional taxes arise when costs below c_1 are realized, i.e., with probability $F(c_1)$. Thus, as is evident from (3.13), the optimal mark-up of price above marginal cost is directly proportional to the term $F(c_1)[f(c_1)]^{-1}C_{xc}(x(c_1), c_1)$. Of course, the trade-off between higher taxes and direct losses from productive distortions is not available at $c = c^-$, so the regulator induces the first-best output for $c = c^-$.

3.3. The role of capital

In this section we examine how the regulatory policy discussed in the previous section would change if the regulator were able to observe the quantity of capital used by the firm. To incorporate capital in the analysis, suppose the firm has a production function of the form

$$x = h(y, \mathbf{z}, c),$$

where y denotes capital and $\mathbf{z} = (z_1, \ldots, z_n)$ denotes a vector of non-capital inputs used by the firm. The neo-classical production function $h(\cdot)$ is assumed to satisfy:

Assumption 3.12 $h_y > 0$; $h_{z_i} > 0$, $i = 1, \ldots, n$.

Assumption 3.13 $h_c < 0$.

Assumption 3.12 states that increases in capital or any non-capital input increase output. Assumption 3.13 indicates that higher realizations of the parameter c reduce the output attainable from any input combination. Thus, as in the previous discussion, higher c realizations imply higher costs of production.

The price of capital to the firm is r per unit and the price vector for z will be denoted by w. The regulator is able to observe y; he also knows r, w, and the functional form of $h(\cdot)$. However, the realizations of c and the quantities of the non-capital inputs used can only be observed by the firm.

Because demand is nonstochastic and known to the regulator, the regulatory policy can be thought of as follows. The firm is faced with a schedule $\{x(c), T(c), y(c)\}$. Each of the three functions in the schedule is indexed by the cost parameter, c. The firm then chooses a particular output- tax- and capital stock-triple from the schedule. (Note that the associated regulated price is determined by $p(c) = P(x(c))$.) After purchasing the selected level of capital $y(c)$ and paying the tax $T(c)$, the firm chooses the unobservable variable inputs (efficiently) to minimize the incremental costs of producing the chosen output, $x(c)$. The minimum incremental costs of producing output x with capital y and cost parameter c is denoted $Z(x, y, c)$, and will be referred to as the firm's *variable cost function*. Assumption 3.12 implies that $Z_x > 0$, $Z_y < 0$. Assumption 3.13 implies that $Z_c > 0$. That is, variable costs increase in output, decrease as more capital is installed, and increase with the cost parameter c. In addition we assume:

Assumption 3.15 $Z_{xc} > 0$.

Assumption 3.16 $Z_{yc} < 0$.

Assumption 3.17 $Z_{yy} > 0$.

Assumption 3.15 is analogous to Assumption 3.8; it states that marginal variable cost increases with c. Assumption 3.16 implies that an increase in c increases the rate at which variable costs fall as more capital is employed. Loosely speaking, this implies that an increase in c will induce the firm to substitute capital for the other unobservable inputs.[9] Assumption 3.17 indicates there are diminishing returns to capital.

---

[9] Only the direction, and not the existence, of capital distortions depends on Assumption (3.16). If $Z_{yc} > 0$, under-capitalization rather than over-capitalization would be optimal.

The optimal regulatory policy can now be found by solving the following problem, [RP-Y].

$$\text{Maximize} \quad \int_{c^-}^{\bar{c}} \{\beta[V(x(c)) - P(x(c))x(c) + T(c)]$$

$$+ [1 - \beta][\pi(c) - \bar{\pi}]\}f(c)\, dc, \quad (3.16)$$

subject to:

$$\pi(c) \geq \bar{\pi}, \qquad \forall\, c \in [c^-, c^+]. \quad (3.17)$$

$$\pi(c) \geq x(\hat{c})P(x(\hat{c})) - T(\hat{c}) - Z(x(\hat{c}), y(\hat{c}), c) - ry(\hat{c}),$$

$$\forall\, c, \hat{c} \in [c^-, c^+] \quad (3.18)$$

$$c^- \leq \bar{c} \leq c^+, \quad (3.19)$$

where

$$\pi(c) \equiv x(c)P(x(c)) - T(c) - Z(x(c), y(c), c) - ry(c).$$

Constraint (3.17) is the individual rationality condition analogous to (3.6), and constraint (3.18) is the self-selection constraint which corresponds to (3.7).

Using techniques developed in Section 3.2, the solution to [RP-Y] can be characterized as follows:

PROPOSITION 3.3 *The solution to* [RP-Y] *has the following three properties:*

i) $p(c) = Z_x(x(c), y(c), c) + H(c)Z_{xc}(x(c), y(c), c)$;

ii) $y(c) > Y^*(x(c), c)$ *for* $c \in (c^-, \bar{c}]$.
   $y(c) = Y^*(x(c^-), c^-)$, *where*
   $Y^*(x, c) = \operatorname*{argmin}_{y}\{Z(x, y, c) + ry\}$; *and*

iii) $\bar{c} = \min(c'', c^+)$, *where* c'' *is the solution to:*
   $V(x(c'')) - Z(x(c''), y(c''), c'') - H(c'')Z_c(x(c''), y(c''), c'')$
   $- ry(c'') - \bar{\pi} = 0$.

The important finding here is that the optimal regulatory policy induces the firm to over-capitalize, i.e., to use a quantity of capital that exceeds the cost-minimizing quantity, given the firm's technology and the output it produces. This conclusion stems from the assumption that $Z_{yc} < 0$. The assumption implies that the lower is the realization of c, the smaller is the cost-minimizing amount of capital for any output level. Consequently, by inducing a capital choice in excess of the cost-minimizing level for high c realizations, it becomes less attractive for the firm to act as if c is high when c is actually low. In effect, the capital distortion lowers the difference in total production costs according to the realization of c. Consequently, the rents that must be awarded the firm when the realized value of c is small are reduced. The parallels between the role of capital distortions and quantity distortions should be apparent.[10]

The similarity between the over-capitalization result in Proposition 3.3 and the over-capitalization result in the Averch–Johnson [2] model of rate-of-return regulation raises the question of whether the optimal regulatory policy resembles rate-of-return regulation in any way. In a model similar to the one presented here, Besanko [16] demonstrates that the optimal regulatory policy can be implemented by a form of "non-linear" rate-of-return regulation in which the allowed rate-of-return varies inversely with the amount of capital the firm employs. By setting a rate-of-return in excess of the cost of capital, the regulator induces the desired degree of overcapitalization; but in order to limit the firm's incentive to overcapitalize "too much," the allowed-rate-of-return decreases with the amount of capital employed.

3.4. Conclusions

This section has discussed several simple models of regulatory pricing under adverse selection. The regulator was presumed able to set prices, taxes and levels of capital investment. However, he was unable to observe realized production costs. In particular, no auditing of the firm's performance was permitted. The purpose of Section 4 is to determine how auditing of production costs can be employed to reduce the distortions arising from the adverse selection problem.

4. AUDITING

In this section, we determine how the optimal regulatory policy changes when the regulator has access to an imperfect monitor of

---

[10] For other models in which particular input distortions arise to limit the rents from private information, see [17], [47], and [75].

the firm's costs. The analysis begins with an extension of the simple binary setting introduced in Section 3. The continuous case is then examined in Section 4.2.

4.1 The binary case

As in Section 3.1, we consider a setting where the firm knows the realization of a critical cost parameter $c \in \{c_L, c_H\}$ while the regulator knows only its distribution and the functional form of the firm's cost function, $C(x, c)$.[11] Assumptions 3.1–3.4 from the binary analysis in Section 3 will be assumed to hold here. Thus, higher realizations of c signal higher total and marginal costs of production.

To capture the possibility that the regulator can "audit" the firm's realized costs, we assume that for a fixed fee, A, the regulator can observe the realization of a random variable, $s \in \{s_L, s_H\}$. This signal is of potential value to the regulator because it is correlated with c. In other words, the conditional probability that $c = c_i$ is greater if $s = s_i$ than if $s = s_j$ for $j \neq i$, $i, j \in \{L, H\}$. This fact is captured formally by Assumption 4.1, where ϕ_{ij} represents the joint probability that $c = c_i$ and $s = s_j$.

Assumption 4.1 $\phi_{ii}[\phi_{Li} + \phi_{Hi}]^{-1} > \phi_{ij}[\phi_{Lj} + \phi_{Hj}]^{-1}$,
                for $j \neq i$, $i, j \in \{L, H\}$.

In this setting the regulator must decide whether to audit the firm's *reported* costs. He must also specify how the firm's compensation will depend upon both reported costs and the outcome of the audit. We assume the firm can (costlessly) communicate its private information (i.e., report its costs) to the regulator before production occurs. Furthermore, we assume the regulator can audit the firm's report before prices are set and production takes place. Thus, production patterns as well as compensation to the firm can be based on the outcome of the audit.

To state the regulator's problem formally, the following notation is helpful. First, let p_{ij} and T_{ij} be the regulated price and tax, respectively, when the firm reports its cost parameter to be c_i and

---

[11] The analysis in this section is based on the works of [4] and [25].

the audit (publicly) reveals $s = s_j$, $i, j \in \{L, H\}$. The corresponding output is $x_{ij} \equiv X(p_{ij})$. The probability that an audit will be conducted when $c = c_i$ is reported by the firm is denoted a_i. If no audit occurs, p_i and T_i will be the regulated price and tax, respectively, when the firm reports $c = c_i$. Given this notation, the regulator's problem, [RP-BA], is to choose prices, taxes and audit probabilities to:

Maximize $\displaystyle\sum_{i=L}^{H} [\phi_{iL} + \phi_{iH}] \Big\{ \sum_{j=L}^{H} a_i \{ \phi_{ij} [\phi_{iL} + \phi_{iH}]^{-1} \{ \beta [S(p_{ij}) + T_{ij}]$

$$+ [1 - \beta] \pi(p_{ij}, T_{ij}; c_i) \} - A \} + [1 - a_i] \{ \beta [S(p_i) + T_i]$$

$$+ [1 - \beta] \pi(p_i, T_i; c_i) \} \Big\},$$

subject to:

$$a_i \Big\{ \sum_{j=L}^{H} \phi_{ij} [\phi_{iL} + \phi_{iH}]^{-1} \pi(p_{ij}, T_{ij}; c_i) \Big\}$$

$$+ [1 - a_i] \pi(p_i, T_i; c_i) \geq \bar{\pi}, \qquad i \in \{L, H\}; \quad (4.1)$$

$$a_i \Big\{ \sum_{j=L}^{H} \phi_{ij} [\phi_{iL} + \phi_{iH}]^{-1} \pi(p_{ij}, T_{ij}; c_i) \Big\} + [1 - a_i] \pi(p_i, T_i; c_i)$$

$$\geq a_k \Big\{ \sum_{j=L}^{H} \phi_{ij} [\phi_{iL} + \phi_{iH}]^{-1} \pi(p_{kj}, T_{kj}; c_i) \Big\} + [1 - a_k] \pi(p_k, T_k; c_i),$$

$$k \neq i, \quad i, k \in \{L, H\}; \quad (4.2)$$

where

$$\pi(p_{ij}, T_{ij}; c_k) \equiv p_{ij} x_{ij} - C(x_{ij}, c_k) - T_{ij}.$$
$$\pi(p_i, T_i; c_k) \equiv p_i x_i - C(x_i, c_k) - T_i.$$

As in Section 3, the individual rationality constraints (4.1) require that the firm's profit exceed the reservation profit $\bar{\pi}$. The self-selection constraints (4.2) ensure that the firm will truthfully announce its cost parameter.

Our focus on regulatory policies that induce truthful reporting by the firm is without loss of generality. This fact is implied by the Revelation Principle (see [21], [39], or [59]). In the regulatory context studied here, where the regulator is able to precommit himself to faithfully execute the terms of any announced policy, the

Revelation Principle implies that for any arbitrary regulatory policy, there exists an alternative policy, which yields the same outcomes and induces the firm to report its cost parameter truthfully. To see why the Revelation Principle holds, consider an arbitrary regulatory policy $M = \{M_L, M_H\}$ where $M_i \equiv (p_i, T_i, p_{ik}, T_{ik}, a_i)$ represents the price-tax-audit combination that is implemented when the firm reports $c = c_i$ and the audit (if conducted) reveals signal s_k. Suppose that under policy M, the firm with cost parameter c_i prefers that M_j be implemented and therefore reports its cost parameter to be c_j, where $i \neq j$ and $i, j \in \{L, H\}$. Suppose, now, that the regulator offered an alternative regulatory policy $\tilde{M} = \{\tilde{M}_L, \tilde{M}_H\}$ where $\tilde{M}_L = M_H$ and $\tilde{M}_H = M_L$. Under this alternative policy if a firm reports c_L (respectively, c_H), M_H (respectively, M_L) will be implemented. Given the firm's preferred reporting strategy under M, it is apparent that the firm will report its cost parameter truthfully under $\tilde{M}$. From the regulator's point of view, policies M and $\tilde{M}$ yield the same outcomes. Consequently there is no loss of generality if we assume that the regulator adopts the "truth-telling" policy, $\tilde{M}$. Although the argument here is in the context of a binary setting, the logic extends in a straightforward manner to more general settings.

If there were no information asymmetry regarding the firm's technology, the regulator would effect the first-best solution to [RP-BA].

DEFINITION 4.1 The first-best solution to [RP-BA] is that in which for $i \in \{L, H\}$:

  i) $\pi(p_i, T_i; c_i) = \bar{\pi}$;
  ii) $p_i = C_x(x_i, c_i)$, and;
  iii) $a_i = 0$.

Thus, the outcome most preferred by the regulator is that in which the firm receives no rents, marginal-cost prices are effected, and no auditing occurs. It follows from Proposition 3.1 that this ideal outcome is unåttainable, because if the auditing is not employed, the firm will command rents from its private information. However, Proposition 4.1 reports that the regulator can come arbitrarily close to achieving the first-best solution.

PROPOSITION 4.1 *Under Assumptions* 3.1–3.4 *and* 4.1, *a feasible solution to* [RP-BA] *is that in which:*

  i) $\pi(p_i, T_i; c_i) = \bar{\pi}$ *for* $i \in \{L, H\}$;

  ii) $p_i = p_{iL} = p_{iH} = C_x(x_i, c_i)$ *for* $i \in \{L, H\}$;

  iii) $a_1 = 0$ *and* $a_2 > 0$ *is arbitrarily close to zero.*

A formal proof of Proposition 4.1 is not very enlightening, and therefore is omitted. The logic behind the proof, however, is worthy of explanation. The essential point is that the risk-neutral firm can be faced with a lottery when it reports $c = c_H$ that is so unattractive if (and only if) the report is false that the firm will never misrepresent its costs. This is the case even if the lottery is effected with arbitrarily small probability. The lottery places a large tax on the firm if the audit reveals $s = s_L$, and compensates the firm with a large subsidy if the audit corroborates the report of "high costs." (For a closely related insight see, for example, [63].)

Of course, the magnitude of the lottery (i.e., the value of $T_{HH} - T_{HL}$) necessary to effect the solution recorded in Proposition 4.1 will be immense. In practice, the penalty that a firm can be forced to pay is limited. For example, bankruptcy laws may limit a firm's liability to the value of its assets. This suggests that important constraints on the firm's liability have been omitted in the formulation of [RP-BA]. Hence, the following reformulation is introduced.

DEFINITION 4.2 [RP-BA]' is the regulator's problem in the binary environment with auditing, [RP-BA], with the additional constraints, (4.3) and (4.4), imposed:

$$\pi(p_{ij}, T_{ij}; c_i) \geq B, \qquad i, j \in \{L, H\}. \tag{4.3}$$

$$\pi(p_i, T_i; c_i) \geq B, \qquad i \in \{L, H\}. \tag{4.4}$$

These constraints put a lower bound on the firm's realized profit. As noted above, B might be the value of the firm's assets. Alternatively, B might represent a mandated fair rate-of-return on invested capital less some legislated maximum fine the firm can be forced to bear when it is found to have misrepresented its costs to the regulator.

PROPOSITION 4.2 *Suppose Assumptions 3.1–3.4 and 4.1 hold, B is finite, and A is sufficiently small that auditing is employed with strictly positive probability. Then the solution to* [RP-BA]' *has the following properties*:

   i) $a_L = 0$;
     $a_H \in (0, 1)$.

  ii) $\pi(p_{HL}, T_{HL}; c_H) = \pi(p_H, T_H; c_H) = B$.

 iii) $E\pi(c_H; c_H) = \bar{\pi}$;
     $E\pi(c_L; c_L) = E\pi(c_H; c_L)$.

 iv) $p_L = C_x(x_L, c_L)$.

  v) $p_H = C_x(x_H, c_H) + \theta_{LH}\{\beta[\phi_{HL} + \phi_{HH}]\}^{-1}$
      $\times [C_x(x_H, c_H) - C_x(x_H, c_L)]$;

$$p_{Hj} = C_x(x_{Hj}, c_H) + \theta_{LH}\phi_{Lj}\{\beta\phi_{Hj}[\phi_{LL} + \phi_{LH}]\}^{-1}$$
$$\times [C_x(x_{Hj}, c_H) - C_x(x_{Hj}, c_L)], \quad j \in \{L, H\},$$

where

$$E\pi(c_i; c_j) \equiv a_i \sum_{k=L}^{H} \phi_{jk}[\phi_{jL} + \phi_{jH}]^{-1}\pi(p_{ik}, T_{ik}; c_j)$$
$$+ [1 - a_i]\pi(p_i, T_i; c_j),$$

and

$$\theta_{LH} \in (0, [\phi_{LL} + \phi_{LH}][2\beta - 1]]).$$

Proposition 4.2, whose proof can be found in Demski *et al.* [25], highlights the essential features of the optimal auditing policy. As is the case without auditing, the incentive problem is to prevent the firm from exaggerating its costs. This is best accomplished by auditing a report of "high costs" (c_H) and imposing the maximum penalty if the audit does not verify the claim (i.e., if s_L is observed). The profit of the firm is also kept to a minimum (B) when high costs are reported and no audit occurs. When $B < \bar{\pi}$, the profit required to induce the firm with high costs to produce is provided when an audit corroborates the firm's claim that $c = c_H$ (i.e., when s_H is observed). In as much, the greatest payoff for a report that $c = c_H$ is made under the outcome $(s = s_H)$ that is least likely when $c = c_L$. Hence, the gains to the firm from exaggerating costs are minimized. Note that a costly audit of a report of low costs $(c = c_L)$ will never be conducted, because the firm has no incentive to understate costs.

Output levels are also designed to limit the rents the firm might achieve by exaggerating costs. This fact is made apparent by Corollary 4.1.

COROLLARY 4.1   *If $C_{xx}(x, c) \geq 0$, and the conditions of Proposition 4.2 hold, then $p_{HL} > p_H > p_{HH}$.*

Proof Suppose $p_{HH} \geq p_H$. Then $x_H \geq x_{HH}$, which implies $C_x(x_{HH}, c_H) - C_x(x_{HH}, c_L) \leq C_x(x_H, c_H) - C_x(x_H, c_L)$ by Assumption 3.4. Also, $C_x(x_{HH}, c_H) \leq C_x(x_H, c_H)$ since $C_{xx}(x, c) \geq 0$, and $\phi_{LH}\{\phi_{HH}[\phi_{LL} + \phi_{LH}]\}^{-1} < [\phi_{HL} + \phi_{HH}]^{-1}$ by Assumption 4.1. Thus, from condition (v) in Proposition 4.2, $p_H > p_{HH}$, which is a contradiction.

The proof that $p_{HL} > p_H$ is analogous.

As noted in Section 3, reducing the output associated with a report of high costs limits the rents to the firm when $c = c_L$, because less output ensures a smaller differential in total production costs according to whether $c = c_H$ or $c = c_L$. Corollary 4.1 reflects the observation that this method of limiting rents will be exploited most heavily for the outcome $(s = s_L)$ that is most likely if $c = c_L$, thereby limiting the firm's anticipated gains from cost exaggeration.

Finally, note from condition (iii) of Proposition 4.2 that for truthfully reporting $c = c_L$, the firm is afforded the minimal increment in profit above what it could secure by exaggerating costs. Again, this feature of the optimal auditing policy follows from the fact that the binding incentive constraint for the regulator is to prevent the firm from exaggerating its costs.

4.2. Auditing with a continuum of types

In this section we discuss a model of auditing with a continuum of possible cost realizations. The focus of the discussion is on the auditing model of Baron and Besanko [7]. In that model, the firm's total cost of production, $\tilde{C}$, is assumed to be stochastic with distribution $h(C \mid c)$ where c represents the firm's private information. As in Section 3.2, c may take on any value in the interval $[c^-, c^+]$. Higher values of c correspond to higher total costs for the firm in the sense of first-order stochastic dominance. The support of $\tilde{C}$ is independent of c.[12]

---

[12] Actually, an alternative interpretation of this set-up is possible. Instead of random production costs and a perfect monitor of realized costs, production costs could be taken to be deterministic while the monitor is stochastic. The insights derived from the two interpretations are analogous when the firm is risk neutral. We choose to discuss the case of stochastic costs for variety. In Section 5, we examine the differences between the two interpretations when the firm is risk averse, and when moral hazard considerations are present.

As in Section 3.2, the regulator is assumed to announce a schedule $\{p(c), T(c)\}$ of price-tax combinations. In addition, however, the regulator specifies an audit probability, $a(c)$. To conduct an audit the regulator incurs a fixed cost A. If the firm is audited following a report of c and costs C are observed, a fine $N(C, c)$ is imposed on the firm.[13] This fine is bounded above by $\bar{N}$ and below by zero.

The regulator's problem, [RP-CA], can be stated as[14,15]

Maximize $\displaystyle\int_{c^-}^{c^+} \{S(p(c)) + T(c) + a(c)E[N(\bar{C}, c) \mid c]$

$$- a(c)A + [1 - \beta]\beta^{-1}\pi(c)\}f(c)\, dc.$$

subject to:

$$\pi(c) \geq p(\hat{c})X(p(\hat{c})) - C(X(p(\hat{c})), c) - T(\hat{c})$$
$$- E[N(\bar{C}, \hat{c}) \mid c] \quad \forall c, \hat{c} \in [c^-, c^+], \quad (4.5)$$

$$\pi(c) \geq 0 \quad \forall c \in [c^-, c^+], \quad (4.6)$$

where

$$\pi(c) \equiv p(c)X(p(c)) - C(X(p(c)), c) - T(c) - E[N(\bar{C}, c) \mid c].$$

$E[N(\bar{C}, \hat{c}) \mid c]$ is the expected value of the fine when $\hat{c}$ is reported and c is the actual value of the firm's cost parameter. $C(x, c)$ is the expectation of total cost when output x is produced and the firm's cost parameter is c.

Constraints (4.5) are the self-selection constraints and (4.6) are the individual rationality constraints.

The next proposition summarizes the optimal regulatory policy with auditing for the case in which

$$\bar{C} = \tilde{\Gamma}x + K. \quad (4.7)$$

Here, $\tilde{\Gamma}$ is a normally distributed random variable with mean c and

---

[13] The Baron and Besanko [7] model is a single-period model and the firm is assumed to have produced before C is realized. Thus, the price $p(c)$ cannot be revised after the audit takes place.

[14] To simplify notation, we focus on solutions in which the firm is induced to produce for all realizations of $c \in [c^-, c^+]$.

[15] Note that in writing the objective function, we have divided through by the weight β given to consumers' surplus.

precision τ, and K is a non-stochastic fixed cost. This example depicts a setting in which higher realizations of c correspond to stochastically higher marginal costs of production.[16]

PROPOSITION 4.3   *Under Assumptions 3.5 and 3.6 and the specification of total costs in (4.7), the solution to* [RP-CA] *has the following features:*[17]

$$p(c) = c + H(c);$$

$$a(c) = \begin{cases} 0 & for \quad c \in [c^-, c_a], \\ 1 & for \quad c \in [c_a, c^+]; \end{cases}$$

$$N(C, c) = \begin{cases} \bar{N} & for \quad C \le cX(p(c)) + K, \\ 0 & for \quad C > cX(p(c)) + K; \end{cases}$$

where c_a is defined by

$$\tau\bar{N}H(c_a) = A\sqrt{2\Pi}, \tag{4.8}$$

and $H(c) = [2\beta - 1]\beta^{-1}F(c)[f(c)]^{-1}$.

Under the optimal regulatory policy with auditing, the regulator audits a firm's costs if its reported cost, c, is sufficiently high (i.e., $c \ge c_a$). Once a firm is audited, however, it is penalized if its total cost is less than the expected total cost given the reported type. The optimal auditing policy can be interpreted as a commitment by the regulator to force the firm to give refunds to consumers if observed costs are lower than expected, given the firm's reported information. Intuitively, this policy is sensible given the firm's incentive to overstate the true value of its cost parameter and the absence of moral hazard.[18] High cost reports trigger an audit; and if the investigation provides evidence that costs were actually low, the

---

[16] Note that the expected cost function $C(x, c)$ corresponding to the specification in (4.7) satisfies Assumptions 3.7–3.11. Thus, there is no need to repeat these assumptions in this section. Assumptions 3.5 and 3.6 from the previous section are explicitly maintained, though.

[17] For Proposition 4.3 to hold an additional regularity condition is needed. This condition is

$$X(c^+ + H(c^+)) \ge \bar{N}/\sqrt{2\Pi},$$

where $\Pi = 3.14159\ldots$ If this regularity condition is not satisfied the expressions for $p(c)$ and c_a are slightly different from those stated in the proposition.

[18] Moral hazard is discussed in the next section.

firm is penalized. It is the risk neutrality of both the regulator and the firm which guarantees the maximum penalty is always imposed if an exaggeration of costs is "detected" by the monitor.

The following corollary states some comparative statics results on the auditing region. To capture the effects of increasing uncertainty, the regulator's priors can be represented by the distribution function $F(c) = [c\sigma[\sigma + 1]^{-1}]^\sigma$, where $c \in [0, 1 + \sigma^{-1}]$. For this distribution, a decrease in σ represents a mean-preserving spread. In this setting, $H(c) = [2\beta - 1]\beta^{-1}c\sigma^{-1}$, and larger values of σ correspond to smaller uncertainty on the part of the regulator about the firm's cost parameter c.

COROLLARY 4.2 *Under the conditions of Proposition* 4.3, *when* $F(c) = [c\sigma[\sigma + 1]^{-1}]^\sigma$ *the regulator audits more often (i.e.,* c_a *falls) as:* (i) *the precision* τ *of the distribution of total cost increases;* (ii) *the regulator's priors become more diffuse (i.e.,* σ *decreases);* (iii) *the maximum allowable penalty* $\bar{N}$ *increases;* (iv) *the cost A of auditing decreases;* (v) *the regulator places a larger weight* β *on consumers' surplus.*

These results are quite intuitive and are readily derived from straightforward differentiation of (4.8). The conclusions indicate that the demand for auditing is strongest when the regulator's initial uncertainty is large and when the result of the audit is very informative about the firm's private information. The same is true when the firm can be penalized heavily following an unfavorable audit, because the auditing instrument is a particularly powerful deterrent against cost exaggeration in this case. Of course, the demand for auditing will also be greater when an investigation of the firm's costs is less expensive and when the regulator is more concerned about consumers' surplus than profit.

5. REGULATION AND MORAL HAZARD

Moral hazard refers to a situation in which one party in a contractual relationship can unilaterally undertake actions that cannot be monitored and controlled by other parties in the relationship. In a regulatory setting, moral hazard can take a variety of forms. For example, if allowed revenues depend on observed costs, the regulated firm may have an incentive to inflate costs.[19] As another example, if it is costly for the firm (or its managers) to acquire information related to input prices or the likely impact of cost-reducing activities, the firm may have an incentive to shirk on the acquisition of such information. In designing regulatory policy, incentives for opportunistic behavior on the part of the firm must be taken into account. In this section, we consider several models in the recent literature that focus on regulatory policy when concerns about both moral hazard and adverse selection are present. Section 5.1 examines the design of optimal auditing policies when the firm must be motivated to engage in cost-reducing activities. Section 5.2 discusses the design of regulatory policy when the firm must be motivated to acquire valuable technological information.

5.1. Auditing and moral hazard

This section discusses the design of regulatory policy when the regulator can audit the firm's costs and the firm makes an "effort" decision that affects the level of costs. The basis of the discussion in this section is the work of Laffont and Tirole [44]. The regulated firm is assumed to have a marginal cost given by $c - e$ where $c \in [c^-, c^+]$ is an unobservable parameter known to the firm but not to the regulator, and e is the effort exerted by the firm. The expenditure of effort entails a non-pecuniary disutility $D(e)$ which satisfies the following assumptions.

Assumption 5.1 The disutility of effort, $D(e)$, is increasing and convex in e; i.e., $D' > 0$ and $D'' \geq 0$.

Assumption 5.2 The rate of which the marginal disutility of effort increases with e is an increasing function of e; i.e. $D''' \geq 0$.

Assumption 5.1 is a standard assumption in the moral hazard literature. It implies that the firm is effort averse and that the marginal disutility of effort increases with effort. Assumption 5.2 is a common regularity condition.

---

[19] Baron and DeBondt [11] present a model of optimal fuel adjustment clauses in which such an incentive must be counteracted.

The firm's total cost is given by:

$$\bar{C} = (c - e)x + K + \bar{\delta}, \tag{5.1}$$

where K is a fixed cost, x is output, and $\bar{\delta} \in [\delta^-, \delta^+]$ is a random disturbance whose expected value is zero and whose density is denoted $g(\bar{\delta})$. In the discussion in this section, the fixed cost K is assumed to be known to the regulator and independent of e.[20]

The regulator is presumed to have the authority to set a price and a tax. Rather than characterizing the price and tax explicitly, Laffont and Tirole state the regulatory policy in terms of an allowed revenue $R(C, \hat{c})$ and an output $x(\hat{c})$, where $\hat{c}$ is the reported value of the firm's cost parameter. As in Baron and Besanko's [7] model of auditing, price is assumed to be set *ex ante,* so output does not depend on the total cost realization C. However, the tax can be adjusted *ex post*; thus, allowed revenue R can depend on both the report, $\hat{c}$, and the realization of total cost, C. Unlike Baron and Besanko's model, there is no upper bound on the *ex post* adjustment in the firm's tax, and auditing is presumed costless. Thus, the regulator will always elect to audit for any cost report.

The regulator's problem, [RP-MH], can be written as:

$$\text{Maximize} \quad \int_{c^-}^{c^+} \{\beta[V(x(c)) - E[R(\bar{C}, c) \mid c, e(c)]]$$
$$+ [1 - \beta]\pi(c)\}f(c)\,dc,$$

subject to:

$$\{c, e(c)\} = \operatorname*{argmax}_{e, \hat{c}} E[R(\bar{C}, \hat{c}) \mid c, e] - [c - e]x(\hat{c}) - K - D(e),$$
$$\tag{5.2}$$

and

$$\pi(c) \equiv E[R(\bar{C}, c) \mid c, e(c)] - [c - e(c)]x(c) - K - D(e(c)) \geq \bar{\pi}.$$
$$\tag{5.3}$$

Here, $V(x)$ denotes consumers' total willingness to pay for x units of output (recall from Section 3.2 that $V(x) = \int_0^x P(t)\,dt$ where $P(\cdot)$ denotes the inverse demand curve). Also, $E[R(C, \hat{c}) \mid c, e]$

---

[20] Laffont and Tirole [44] also consider the case in which fixed costs depend on effort. The results in this case are not very different from the case discussed here.

denotes the expected revenue of the firm when it puts forth effort e, reports cost realization, $\hat{c}$, and has actual cost c; i.e.,

$$E[R(\bar{C}, \hat{c}) \mid c, e] = \int_{\delta^-}^{\delta^+} R([c - e]x(\hat{c}) + K + \delta, \hat{c})g(\delta)\,d\delta.$$

Constraint (5.2) is the standard self-selection constraint; it indicates that the optimal policy induces truthful reporting and also defines an effort response function $e(c)$. Condition (5.3) is the individual rationality constraint.

As a benchmark we will state the effort and quantity of output that the regulator would implement if he knew the firm's cost parameter c and could observe and dictate the choice of effort.

DEFINITION 5.1 The first-best solution to [RP-MH] is a revenue function, $R^*(c)$, quantity of output, $x^*(c)$, and amount of effort, $e^*(c)$, given by:

$$R^*(c) = [c - e^*(c)]x^*(c) + D(e^*(c)) + K + \bar{\pi}, \qquad (5.4)$$

$$P(x^*(c)) = c - e^*(c), \qquad (5.5)$$

$$D'(e^*(c)) = x^*(c). \qquad (5.6)$$

Relation (5.4) simply states that the firm receives no rents. Relation (5.5) indicates that output will be chosen to equate price and marginal cost. And relation (5.6) defines the effort choice as that which equates the marginal disutility of effort to its marginal benefit in terms of cost reductions.

Both the regulator and the firm are assumed to be risk-neutral. Therefore, if the regulator knew the cost parameter c, the first-best solution could be achieved even if effort were unobservable. This is a special case of a well-known result in the principal-agent literature that in the absence of adverse selection, the moral hazard problem disappears when both the principal and the agent are risk neutral. (See, for example, [38] or [41].)

PROPOSITION 5.1 *When there is moral hazard but no adverse selection, the first-best solution to* [RP-MH] *can be achieved without auditing.*

Proof. If the firm is compensated according to the first-best revenue function, $R^*(c)$, the firm chooses effort to maximize:

$$[e - e^*(c)]x^*(c) - [D(e) - D(e^*(c))] + \bar{\pi}.$$

The solution to this problem is the first-best effort, $e^*(c)$. The firm's profit under the policy is $\bar{\pi}$. Thus, the regulator achieves the first-best level of surplus for any value of the cost parameter c.

Proposition 5.1 implies that there is no need to audit the firm if it has no private information about its technological capabilities. Under these circumstances the regulator can order the firm to produce the first-best output. Moreover, because its payment is independent of the realized cost (i.e., a fixed-price contract), the firm reaps all the benefits of its effort, and thus chooses effort to minimize expected production costs.

A second extreme case is that in which there is adverse selection but no moral hazard (i.e., there is no effort put forth by the firm). In this case the assumptions of costless auditing and no bounds on the *ex post* adjustment to the tax imply that the regulator can approximate the first-best solution arbitrarily closely. (Recall Proposition 4.1.). This result is stated as:

PROPOSITION 5.2 *When there is adverse selection but no moral hazard, the regulator can come arbitrarily close to effecting the first-best solution to* [RP-MH].

Proof. Consider the following policy:

$$R(C, c) = B_0(c) + B_1 C,$$

where B_1 is a positive scalar that is arbitrarily close to one, and

$$B_0(c) = [1 - B_1]\left\{ \int_c^{c^+} x(t)\, dt + cx(c) + K \right\} + \bar{\pi}.$$

Furthermore, let output $x(c)$ be given by:

$$P(x(c)) = c + [1 - B_1]H(c),$$

$$\text{where } H(c) = [2\beta - 1]\beta^{-1}F(c)f(c)^{-1}.$$

It is straightforward to verify that this policy satisfies the self-selection constraints. Moreover,

$$\lim_{B_1 \to 1} x(c) = x^*(c), \quad \text{and} \quad \lim_{B_1 \to 1} \pi(c) = \bar{\pi}.$$

Thus, as the cost reimbursement, B_1, approaches one, the regulator's expected surplus approaches the expected value of the surplus generated by the first-best solution.

The intuition behind Proposition 5.2 is that when the firm is reimbursed fully for realized costs, there is no reason for the firm to exaggerate likely costs by overstating c. And if realized costs are independent of effort (i.e., if there is no moral hazard problem), no incentive problem emerges under full reimbursement of realized costs.

Propositions 5.1 and 5.2 help explain the regulator's optimal strategy when he faces a moral hazard problem and an adverse selection problem simultaneously. If there were only a moral hazard problem, the regulator would institute a fixed-price contract under which payment to the firm is independent of realized costs. On the other hand, if there were only an adverse selection problem, he would opt for full cost reimbursement. The next proposition—proven in [44]—indicates that when both problems exist simultaneously, the optimal solution represents a compromise between these two extremes.

PROPOSITION 5.3 *If both a moral hazard and an adverse selection problem are present, the solution to* [RP-MH] *involves a revenue function that can be expressed as a linear function of the realized total cost; i.e.,*

$$R(C, c) = \tilde{B}_0(c) + \tilde{B}_1(c)C.$$

The fraction $\tilde{B}_1(c)$ of costs reimbursed is given by

$$\tilde{B}_1(c) = 1 - D'(e(c))/[D'(e(c)) + D''(e(c))H(c)]. \quad (5.7)$$

Effort $e(c)$ and the quantity $x(c)$ of output are given by

$$P(x(c)) = c - e(c). \quad (5.8)$$

$$D'(e(c)) + D''(e(c))H(c) = x(c). \quad (5.9)$$

This solution is interpreted in Corollaries 5.1–5.3.

COROLLARY 5.1 *For a firm with cost parameter $c > c^-$, the fraction of costs reimbursed is strictly between zero and one. For $c = c^-$, a fixed-price contract is optimal.*

The intuition behind this corollary is straightforward. Because of the moral hazard problem, the regulator will not reimburse the firm fully for realized costs; i.e., $\bar{B}_1(c) < 1$. Full cost reimbursement provides no incentive for cost reduction. However, some cost reimbursement is desirable because, as argued earlier, it counteracts the firm's incentive to exaggerate c. Thus, the conjunction of moral hazard and adverse selection results in a contract with partial cost reimbursement when $c > c^-$.

COROLLARY 5.2 *If both a moral hazard and adverse selection problem are present, the optimal regulatory policy calls for marginal cost pricing,* given *the effort exerted by the firm.*

This result may be surprising. Recall (from Section 3) that when adverse selection is the only problem faced by the regulator, prices in excess of marginal costs are desirable to limit the firm's rents from its private information. When moral hazard is present, however, prices below marginal cost are desirable, as the resulting increase in output increases the marginal benefit from effort, and thereby provides greater incentive for the firm to increase effort. Corollary 5.2 reports that when the firm is risk neutral the countervailing output distortions called for under adverse selection and moral hazard are exactly offsetting, and marginal cost prices are optimal.

Of course, as one might suspect, with partial cost reimbursement the effort exerted by the firm will fall short of the first-best effort level. Consequently, even though price is set equal to realized marginal cost, this cost exceeds the first-best level, so the firm's output will fall short of its first-best level. These observations are recorded formally in the next corollary.

COROLLARY 5.3 *For all but the most efficient producer, effort and output fall short of their first-best levels; i.e., $e(c) < e^*(c)$ and $x(c) < x^*(c)$ for $c > c^-$. For the most efficient producer, effort and output are at their first-best levels; i.e., $e(c^-) = e^*(c^-)$ and $x(c^-) = x^*(c^-)$.*

Additional considerations arise when the regulated firm is risk averse. In this case, studied by Baron and Besanko [10], the terms of the optimal regulatory policy are sensitive to randomness in realized costs and to noise in the auditing technology. In particular, the source of risk is important. If the monitor of the firm's realized costs is relatively accurate, then some of the risk borne by the firm can be eliminated by basing the firm's compensation on the realization of the monitor. On the other hand, when the monitor is very imperfect, basing compensation on the audit can add undue risk.

Baron and Besanko focus on two special cases of this general setting: (1) deterministic costs with an imperfect monitor of realized costs; and (2) random costs with a perfect monitor of realized costs. When costs are deterministic and the monitor is noisy, the first-best arrangement would have the firm bear no risk under a fixed-price contract. As noted above, the moral hazard problem is avoided under such a contract. Consequently, deviations from the first-best arrangement in this setting are designed to mitigate the adverse selection problem, not the moral hazard problem. Two types of deviation are optimal here. First, the firm receives some reimbursement for realized costs. Though such reimbursement worsens risk sharing (because the monitor is noisy) and reduces the effort provided by the firm, it does help alleviate the adverse selection problem. Second, the regulated price is set in excess of marginal cost. As noted in Section 3, prices in excess of marginal cost limit the gains from cost exaggeration, and thus reduce total payments to the firm.

When costs are random and the monitor is deterministic, the first-best arrangement would have the risk-averse firm reimbursed fully for the costs it incurs. Such an arrangement eliminates the adverse selection problem but does a poor job of motivating the firm to exert effort to reduce costs. Consequently, deviations from the first-best arrangement in this setting are designed to counteract the moral hazard problem, not the adverse selection problem. Again, two distortions arise. First, in order to induce greater effort, the firm receives only partial reimbursement for realized costs. Second, the regulated price is set below marginal cost. The resulting increase in output increases the marginal benefit of effort (which reduces unit production costs) and thereby alleviates the moral hazard problem.

5.2. Moral hazard and information acquisition

Not only must a regulated firm often be motivated to undertake actions that directly reduce costs, but it must also be induced to acquire costly information needed to make better production and investment decisions. This section discusses a model of information acquisition with moral hazard presented by Sappington [76].

In Sappington's model, the firm's cost function is given initially by $C(x) = c_H x + K$. With positive probability, marginal costs can be reduced to a lower level c_L by an investment I in cost-reducing activities. The magnitude of the investment is observable to both regulator and firm. The probability that marginal costs will decrease to c_L when I dollars are invested is given by $q(I; \xi)$, where ξ is a random variable taking on values in the set $\{\xi_L, \xi_H\}$. ξ captures information about the productivity of the cost-reducing investment. The firm can observe the realization ξ_i of the random variable ξ by incurring a positive cost. The regulator does not have access to this information nor can it verify whether the firm has acquired the information. The regulator does, however, have some ability to monitor the firm's realized production costs after the investment has been made.

The timing of actions in this model is as follows. The firm initially decides whether to acquire information. The firm is then asked to report the observed realization of ξ to the regulator. (Even if the firm has not acquired the information, it can still claim to have observed one of two values.) Based on the reported information, ξ_i, $i \in \{L, H\}$, the regulator dictates a level of investment I_i and an "intensity" d_i of the ensuing audit. d_i is the probability that the regulator detects a cost reduction given that such a reduction has occurred. Finally, the regulator specifies a price and tax, (p_{iL}, T_{iL}), if the firm reports that it has observed $\xi = \xi_i$ and the audit reveals that a cost reduction has occurred. If cost reduction is not detected, the regulated price and tax are (p_{iH}, T_{iH}). In Sappington's model, the regulator is assumed to be bound by a fair rate-of-return rule. Thus, the firm's profits must be zero, based on observed costs. The firm's actual profits may still be positive, however, because the regulator's ability to detect cost reductions may be imperfect.

The regulator faces two incentive problems in this setting. First, he must motivate the firm to acquire information. Second, he must induce the firm to report this information truthfully once it has been acquired. In the simple binary model considered, however, the second problem turns out to be solved automatically given that the first problem is resolved.

Three features of the regulator's optimal policy in this setting are noteworthy. First, $d_1 < d_2 < 1$. One interpretation of this finding is that the regulator may commit to an imperfect monitoring technology even though a perfect monitor is available at no cost. This occurs because if the regulator were able to detect cost reductions with certainty, a firm's profit would always be zero; consequently, the firm would have no incentive to acquire information.

Second, $p_{iH} < c_H$, for $i \in \{L, H\}$. That is, if the regulator does not detect a cost reduction, he sets price below marginal cost. This price reduction increases output above the efficient level; but it also increases the firm's profit $[c_H - c_L]X(p_{iH})$ when a cost reduction goes undetected, thereby increasing the firm's incentive to acquire the private information ξ.

Third, when favorable information about investment productivity is obtained, the regulator requires the firm to overinvest relative to the first-best investment. An increment in investment yields a larger expected benefit when the firm has observed favorable information than when the firm is uninformed. Therefore, by increasing the required investment beyond its efficient level, the regulator makes it less attractive for the firm to remain uninformed and simply claim to have observed the favorable signal.

5.3. Conclusions

This section of the monograph has examined two models of moral hazard. In the first model, the firm must be motivated to make an unobservable effort that affects realized production costs directly. In the second model, the firm must be motivated to acquire investment-related information. In both models, the simultaneous presence of moral hazard and adverse selection leads to optimal policies that are quite different from the optimal policies if either moral hazard or adverse selection were the only problem faced by the regulator. Moreover, policies that do a good job of dealing with one problem (e.g., prices in excess of marginal cost in the case of adverse selection) may be quite inappropriate when the other problem (moral hazard) is present. This discussion serves to emphasize the complexity of the incentive problems faced by a regulator when there is imperfect information. It also points out the difficulty of making policy prescriptions that address one, but not both, of the incentive problems that arise under imperfect information.[21]

6. MULTIPERIOD MODELS OF REGULATION AND INFORMATION

In previous sections we analyzed models of regulatory pricing in which the interaction between the regulatory authority and the regulated firm is not repeated. In practice, however, regulation generally involves an ongoing relationship between the regulator and the firm. In such a continuing relationship, the set of policy alternatives available to the regulator is richer because he can base current policies on previous behavior and performance. Under such a regime, however, the firm may have an incentive to alter current behavior in order to affect future regulations. To illustrate, if a firm that demonstrates good compliance with current standards is automatically saddled with more stringent future standards, the firm will reduce current compliance so as to secure more lenient future standards.[22]

This section presents two models of repeated regulatory interactions. In Section 6.1, the binary model of adverse selection presented in Section 3.1 is generalized to a two-period setting. The optimal two-period policy is similar to the optimal single-period policy; however, the adverse selection problem in the second period may be less severe. Some thoughts on the continuous version of the two-period model are also presented in Section 6.1.

In Section 6.2 we consider the repeated adverse selection problem in an environment where the regulator has much less information about the firm's technology and/or demand structure, but is presumed able to observe total expenditures by the firm. The ability to observe this accounting data can dramatically enhance the regulator's ability to resolve the repeated adverse selection problem.

---

[21] There is another type of moral hazard problem that may arise in a regulatory setting that this section has not addressed: how can the regulator be motivated to exert the appropriate amount of supervisory effort on behalf of consumers? This issue has been examined in a recent paper by Demski and Sappington [24].

[22] This phenomenon, known as the ratcheting problem, will be discussed in Section 7.3.

6.1. Two-period with adverse selection

6.1.1. *The Binary Setting.* The binary model of adverse selection considered in Chapter 3 serves as our starting point in this section. For simplicity we assume the firm's cost function is linear in each of the two periods; i.e.,

$$C(x, c_t) = c_t x + K,$$

where c_t denotes marginal cost in period t, $t = 1, 2$. K is a fixed cost of production that is assumed to be the same in each period, and known to both the regulator and the firm. The first-period marginal cost c_1 is known to the firm, but not to the regulator at the beginning of period one. Neither party observes the realization of second-period marginal cost, c_2, until the start of that period. At that time c_2 is observed only by the firm.

The marginal cost in each period is assumed to take on one of two values in the set $\{c_L, c_H\}$, where $c_H > c_L$.[23] The unconditional probability that marginal cost equals c_i in any period is ϕ_i for $i \in \{L, H\}$, where $\phi_L + \phi_H = 1$. The conditional probability that second-period marginal cost is c_i given that the first-period marginal cost is c_j is denoted $\phi(i; j)$. For each i, j, $0 \le \phi(i; j) \le 1$; and for each $j \in \{L, H\}$, $\phi(L; j) + \phi(H; j) = 1$. The marginal costs will be assumed to be positively correlated over time.

Assumption 6.1 $\phi(i; i) \ge \phi(i; j)$ $j \ne i, \quad i, j \in \{L, H\}$.

Assumption 6.1 indicates, for example, that the likelihood of a low marginal cost in the second period is greater when the marginal cost in the first is low than when it is high. Similarly, it indicates that the likelihood of having a high marginal cost in the second period is enhanced by having a high marginal cost in the first period.

As in the previous sections, the regulator is assumed to have the power to set a price p and levy a lump-sum tax T. No auditing of realized costs is permitted, and the regulator is presumed able to precommit to a two-period regulatory policy. We let p_i and T_i represent the regulated first-period price and tax, respectively, when the firm's first-period marginal cost is c_i, $i \in \{L, H\}$. p_{ij} and T_{ij}

---

[23] Thus, subscripts 1 and 2 refer to the time period, while subscripts L and H refer to the particular cost realization.

will be the corresponding second-period variables when first- and second-period cost realizations are c_i and c_j, respectively. We will also refer to the firm's total compensation.

DEFINITION 6.1   The total compensation (R) to the firm in period t is the difference between total revenue and the tax in period t; i.e.,

$$R_i \equiv p_i X_1(p_i) - T_i, \qquad i \in \{L, H\}.$$
$$R_{ij} \equiv p_{ij} X_2(p_{ij}) - T_{ij}, \qquad i, j \in \{L, H\}.$$

A two-period regulatory policy will hereafter be represented as a specification $\{(R_i, x_i), (R_{ij}, x_{ij})\}$ of a compensation and an output level in each period. Notice that the demand function may change over time, but in a manner that is known throughout to both regulator and firm. The sequence of actions and events in the model is summarized in Figure 6.1.

The optimal regulatory policy is found by solving the following problem, [RP-B2].

$$\text{Maximize} \quad \sum_{i=L}^{H} \{\beta[V(x_i) - R_i] + [1 - \beta][R_i - c_i x_i - K]\}\phi_i$$

$$+ \delta \sum_{i=L}^{H} \sum_{j=L}^{H} \{\beta[V(x_{ij}) - R_{ij}] + [1 - \beta][R_{ij} - c_j x_{ij} - K]\}\phi(j; i)\phi_i$$

$$\tag{6.1}$$

subject to:

$$R_{ij} - c_j x_{ij} - K \geq R_{ik} - c_j x_{ik} - K, \qquad j \neq k, \quad i, j, k \in \{L, H\}; \tag{6.2}$$

$$R_i - c_i x_i - K + \delta\{\pi_{ii}\phi(i; i) + \pi_{ij}\phi(j; i)\} \geq R_k - c_i x_k - K$$
$$+ \delta\{\pi_{ki}\phi(i; i) + \pi_{kk}\phi(k; i)\}, \qquad i \neq k, \quad i, k \in \{L, H\}; \tag{6.3}$$

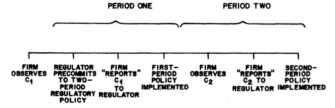

FIGURE 6.1   Sequence of actions and events in the two period binary setting.

$$\pi_{ij} \geq \bar{\pi}, \qquad i, j \in \{L, H\}; \qquad (6.4)$$

$$R_i - c_i x_i - K + \delta\{\pi_{ii}\phi(i; i) + \pi_{ij}\phi(j; i)\} \geq [1 + \delta]\bar{\pi},$$
$$i, j \in \{L, H\}; \quad (6.5)$$

where

$$\pi_{ij} \equiv R_{ij} - c_j x_{ij} - K, \qquad i, j \in \{L, H\}.$$

The variable $\delta \in (0, 1]$ denotes the common discount factor of the firm and the regulator.

Constraints (6.2) are the self-selection constraints for the second period. They are analogous to the self-selection constraints in the single-period problem and simply state that whatever the first-period "cost-report" (c_i), the firm will truthfully reveal second-period realized costs (c_j) for $i, j \in \{L, H\}$. Constraints (6.3) are self-selection constraints for the first period. They ensure that when $c_1 = c_i$ the firm has no incentive to claim that $c_1 = c_j$. These constraints account for the manner in which first-period cost reports affect output and total payment in the second period.[24]

Constraints (6.4) are the individual rationality constraints for the second period, while constraints (6.5) are the individual rationality constraints for the first period. Note that by imposing constraints (6.4), it is implicitly assumed that the firm is always able to "walk away" in the second period (i.e., choose autarky and the reservation profit level, $\bar{\pi}$) regardless of any "promises" it may have made to the regulator in the first period.

The characterization of [RP-B2] proceeds along the same lines as the characterization of the single-period binary model of adverse selection in Section 3.1. Consequently, we simply state the solution to [RP-B2] in the next proposition, omitting a formal proof.

PROPOSITION 6.1 *Under Assumption 6.1, the solution to* [RP-B2] *has the following features:*

i) $R_H - c_H x_H - K + \delta\{\pi_{HL}\phi(L; H) + \pi_{HH}\phi(H; H)\} = [1 + \delta]\bar{\pi}.$

ii) $\pi_{iH} = \bar{\pi}, \qquad i \in \{L, H\}.$

iii) $R_L - c_L x_L - K + \delta\{\pi_{LL}\phi(L; L) + \pi_{LH}\phi(H; L)\}$
$$= R_H - c_L x_H - K + \delta\{\pi_{HL}\phi(L; L) + \pi_{HH}\phi(H; L)\}.$$

---

[24] Our specification of the self-selection constraints in (6.2) and (6.3) is justified by the multiperiod version of the Revelation Principle derived in [87].

iv) $R_{iL} - c_L x_{iL} - K = R_{iH} - c_L x_{iH} - K, \qquad i \in \{L, H\}.$

v) $p_L = P(x_L) = c_L.$

vi) $p_H = P(x_H) = c_H + \phi_L [2\beta - 1][\phi_H \beta]^{-1}[c_H - c_L].$

viii) $p_{iL} = P(x_{iL}) = c_L, \qquad i \in \{L, H\}.$

viii) $p_{LH} = P(x_{LH}) = c_H.$

ix) $p_{HH} = P(x_{HH}) = c_H + \phi_L[2\beta - 1][\phi_H \beta]^{-1}$
$\times [\phi(L; L) - \phi(L; H)][\phi(H; H)]^{-1}.$

The main features of the optimal dynamic regulatory policy are recorded in Corollaries 6.1–6.7. The first two corollaries characterize the first-period regulatory policy, where reference is made to the conclusions of Section 3.1.

COROLLARY 6.1 *In the two-period binary setting, the first-period prices are identical to the prices in the single-period binary model with adverse selection.*

COROLLARY 6.2 *In the two-period binary setting, the first-period taxes (T_L and T_H) are greater than the corresponding taxes in the single-period binary model with adverse selection.*

The regulator can increase the first-period tax in this dynamic setting because there is a positive probability that the firm will have a low marginal cost in the second period ($c_2 = c_L$) and therefore will earn positive profits in that period. The increase in the tax relative to the single-period tax can be interpreted as a franchise fee that the firm must pay for the right to produce in the second period. The reason that only taxes and not first-period prices differ in this dynamic setting is explained following Corollary 6.4.

The next set of corollaries describes the second-period regulatory policy.

COROLLARY 6.3 *The optimal regulatory policy involves marginal cost pricing in the second period except when the firm has high costs in both the first and second periods.*

COROLLARY 6.4 *If $\phi(L; L) < 1$, $p_{HH} - c_H < p_H - c_H$. In other words, when high costs are realized in both periods of the two-period model, the second-period distortion is less pronounced than the first-period distortion.*

Recall from Sections 3.1 and 3.2 that the role of price and output distortions is to better enable the regulator to extract rents from the privately-informed firm. Thus, these distortions will be less pronounced when it is less difficult for the regulator to control the firm's rents. With costs that are imperfectly correlated over time, the firm's information about second-period costs is better than the regulator's information when the regulatory policy is formulated, but it is not perfect. Thus, some second-period distortions will be effected to limit the firm's rents from private information; but the distortions are smaller than in the first period when the relevant information asymmetry is more severe. Of course, as Corollary 6.1 reports, first-period distortions will be exactly as in the single-period model, since the relevant information asymmetry is the same and the firm is risk neutral, so no intertemporal risk-sharing possibilities are relevant.

The explanation of Corollary 6.4 suggests that the degree of distortion should depend in a systematic way on the degree of correlation between costs across period. This intuition is formalized in:

COROLLARY 6.5 *The distortion $(p_{HH} - c_H)$ of price from marginal cost in the second period is an increasing function of the difference $(\phi(L; L) - \phi(L; H))$ in the conditional probability that $c_2 = c_L$.*

The difference $\phi(L; L) - \phi(L; H)$ is a measure of the correlation between marginal costs in the first and second periods. When $\phi(L; L) - \phi(L; H) = 0$, costs are completely uncorrelated across periods. In this case we can state:

COROLLARY 6.6 *If costs are uncorrelated across periods, there is no distortion of price from marginal cost in the second period.*

The intuition behind this conclusion is straightforward. When costs are uncorrelated across periods, the firm and the regulator have symmetric information about second-period costs when the regulator precommits to the regulatory policy. Therefore, the regulator and firm agree on the expected costs of the risk-neutral firm. Consequently, there is no need to distort the second-period prices, since all second-period rents can be extracted from the firm via the "complete decentralization" incentive scheme discussed in Section 3 (p. 8). The opposite extreme is the case of perfectly correlated costs, where $\phi(L; L) = \phi(H; H) = 1$. In this case, we have:

COROLLARY 6.7   *When costs are perfectly correlated across periods, first- and second-period prices are identical, and are given by the prices in the single-period binary model with adverse selection.*

The case of perfect correlation emphasizes the importance of precommitment.[25] With perfect correlation, the regulator deviates from the first-best solution of marginal cost pricing in the second period even though it knows the firm's cost with certainty. With the power to precommit, it is optimal for the regulator to "ignore" the information he acquires in the first period in order to reduce the first-period rents the firm can command from its private information.

6.1.2. *The continuous setting.*   A two-period model of adverse selection has been studied by Baron and Besanko [8] for the case where the critical cost parameter can take on a continuum of values. In their model the regulator's priors are described by distribution functions $F_1(c_1)$ and $F_2(c_2 \mid c_1)$ where $c_t \in [c^-, c^+]$, $t = 1, 2$. The associated density functions are $f_1(c_1)$ and $f_2(c_2 \mid c_1)$, respectively. To formalize the idea that costs are correlated across periods, the following assumption is made:

Assumption 6.2

$$\partial F_2(c_2 \mid c_1)/\partial c_1 < 0, \quad \text{for} \quad c_2 \in (c^-, c^+);$$
$$\partial F_2(c_2 \mid c_1)/\partial c_1 = 0, \quad \text{for} \quad c_2 = c^- \quad \text{and} \quad c_2 = c^+.$$

Assumption 6.2 implies that an increase in c_1 makes higher realizations of c_2 more likely in the sense of first-order stochastic dominance.

The expressions for the first- and second-period prices in the continuous setting are:

$$p_1(c_1) = c_1 + H_1(c_1), \tag{6.6}$$

and

$$p_2(c_1, c_2) = c_2 + H_2(c_1, c_2), \tag{6.7}$$

---

[25] The implications of limited commitment power are studied in the next section.

where

$$H_1(c_1) \equiv [2\beta - 1]\beta^{-1}F_1(c_1)[f_1(c_1)]^{-1}, \tag{6.8}$$

and

$$H_2(c_1, c_2) \equiv -H(c_1)[\partial F_2(c_2 \mid c_1)/\partial c_1][f_2(c_2 \mid c_1)]^{-1}. \tag{6.9}$$

As was the case in the binary setting, the first-period price is identical to the optimal price in a single-period model with adverse selection (see Proposition 3.2). However, the second-period price in the continuous setting is generally more complicated than its counterpart in the binary setting. To illustrate the differences and similarities between the binary and continuous settings, an example is considered.

Suppose that $c_1 \in [0, \infty)$ and c_2 is given by

$$c_2 = c_1^\gamma \varepsilon^{1-\gamma} \tag{6.10}$$

where ε is a random variable that takes on values in the interval $[0, \infty)$ and $\gamma \in [0, 1]$ is a parameter that indexes the strength of the correlation between c_1 and c_2.[26] With the specification in (6.10) one can show that $[\partial F_2/\partial c_1][f_2]^{-1} = -\gamma c_2 c_1^{-1}$. Using (6.7) the second-period price can then be written as

$$p_2(c_1, c_2) = c_2 + \gamma c_2 c_1^{-1}H_1(c_1). \tag{6.11}$$

Notice that the distortion $(\gamma c_2 c_1^{-1}H_1(c_1))$ from marginal cost pricing in the second period may exceed the first-period distortion $(H_1(c_1))$, in contrast to the finding in the binary setting. This difference stems from the fact that in the continuous setting, the regulator has relatively less "flexibility" in manipulating the first- and second-period payments to the firm in order to induce truthful cost reports. The reduced flexibility in the continuous setting arises because of the closer proximity of possible cost realizations, and thus of possible "capabilities" of the firm. Consequently, with reduced *payment* flexibility, the second-period *quantity* distortions that arise in the continuous model may be more severe than the corresponding distortions in the binary setting.

---

[26] Allowing the cost parameter to have positive support on the unbounded interval $[0, \infty)$ rather than on a closed interval facilitates the exposition here without altering the basic insights in any important way.

The continuous and binary models do yield the same results for the "extreme" cases of independent costs and perfectly correlated costs. This general observation is readily observed in the example. When $\gamma = 0$, costs are independent. It is evident from (6.11) that in this case, marginal cost prices will be effected in the second period for any realization of c_2. When $\gamma = 1$, costs are perfectly correlated. In this case $c_1 = c_2$ and (6.11) reduces to

$$p_2(c_1) = c_1 + H_1(c_1),$$

i.e., the first- and second-period prices are identical, as they were in the binary setting with perfect correlation.

6.2. Repeated interactions with observable accounting data

To this point, we have followed much of the literature in presuming the regulator has perfect knowledge of both the demand curve facing the firm and the firm's discount rate, and rather detailed information about the firm's technology. The only source of uncertainty for the regulator was a single technological parameter, whose distribution was common knowledge, but whose realization was known only to the firm. In practice, the regulator's uncertainty may be much more severe. Thus, a question arises as to how a regulator might deal with a repeated adverse selection problem when he has virtually no information concerning the environment in which the firm operates.

Vogelsang and Finsinger (V–F) [88] were among the first to address this question formally. They considered the plight of a regulator who knew only that the firm's vector of n products $\mathbf{x} = (x_1, \ldots, x_n)$ were produced with a technology characterized by decreasing ray average costs (DRAC).

DEFINITION 6.3   The cost function $C(\mathbf{x})$ exhibits decreasing ray average costs if and only if for any scalar $r \geq 1$, $C(r\mathbf{x}) \leq rC(\mathbf{x})$.

Note that if the firm produces only a single product, DRAC implies that average costs of production are everywhere declining.

V–F also presumed that the repeated interaction between regulator and firm took place in a stationary environment; i.e., cost and demand functions are the same in every period. The firm was assumed to have perfect knowledge of these functions and to myopically maximize profit in each period, taking as given the announced regulatory policy. The particular policy proposed by V–F is the following. The firm is permitted to set any price vector $\mathbf{p}_t = (p_{1t}, \ldots, p_{nt})$ it chooses in each period $t = 1, \ldots, \infty$ provided the vector lies within a specified region, R_t, whose definition is

DEFINITION 6.4 $R_t = \{\mathbf{p} \mid \mathbf{p}\mathbf{X}(\mathbf{p}_{t-1}) - E_{t-1} \le 0\}$, where $\mathbf{X}(\mathbf{p}_{t-1}) = (x_{1,t-1}, \ldots, x_{n,t-1})$ and E_{t-1} are the firm's total expenditures in period $t - 1$.

Thus, the V–F scheme awards the firm nearly complete latitude in its pricing decisions. The single overall constraint is that in each period prices must be such that if last period's outputs were sold at these prices, total revenue would not exceed last period's expenditures.

Note that when the firm maximizes profits, production costs are minimized, so $E_t = C(\mathbf{X}_t)$. Note further that implementation of the V–F regulatory mechanism requires that the total expenditures of the firm be observable at the end of each period.

The main conclusion of V–F was that given certain plausible regularity assumptions, if the firm is only required to choose a price vector $\mathbf{p}_t$ in each period such that $\mathbf{p}_t \in R_t$ and serve all demand at those prices, it will choose prices that guarantee a positive increment in total surplus (i.e., consumers' surplus plus profit) in each successive period. Furthermore, the level of total surplus generated in each period converges over time to the level that the regulator would effect if he could set prices with perfect knowledge of cost and demand functions. Intuitively, the V–F scheme forces the firm to lower prices over time in order to secure temporary profit. The assumption of decreasing ray average costs ensures that as prices are lowered in each period, the ensuing increase in demand can be produced at lower "average" cost by the firm. Thus, the firm will not be driven into bankruptcy by the V–F regulatory scheme.

The conclusion of Vogelsang and Finsinger is an important and rather startling one. It states that with only the ability to observe the firm's expenditures but with virtually no knowledge of the (myopic) firm's (static) environment, the firm can eventually be induced with a simple regulatory scheme to set prices in the social interest. Unfortunately, however, the scheme is not immune to strategic behavior by the firm. For example, if the firm acts to maximize the present discounted value of its future stream of profit rather than myopically maximizing profit in each period, it may be advantageous for the firm to waste resources. By spending more than the minimum possible production costs in any period t (i.e., by setting $E_t > C(\mathbf{x}_t)$), the firm can expand the set of feasible prices (R_t) in subsequent periods. And it turns out that the sacrifice of current profit can generate greater (discounted) future profit. This problem of strategic manipulation of the V–F regulatory scheme can be so pronounced that imposition of the scheme may actually reduce the level of the stream of (total) surplus generated below the corresponding stream under an unregulated monopolist.[27]

The use of subsidies can help eliminate strategic behavior of this sort. Loeb and Magat (L–M) [51], for example, considered the value of subsidies in an environment where the regulator and the firm both knew the demand curve facing the firm. The regulator was assumed to know nothing about the firm's production costs. L–M noted that if the firm were awarded a subsidy equal to the level of consumers' surplus generated by its pricing decision, the firm would always act so as to maximize the total surplus. In particular, marginal cost prices would be effected and production costs would be minimized. Furthermore, to ensure this outcome, the interaction between regulator and firm need not be an ongoing one, and the regulator need not observe the firm's expenditures.

Thus, aside from the issue of whether subsidies can be raised costlessly, there are only two drawbacks to the L–M scheme: the requirement that the demand function be known to the regulator, and the distribution of surplus that results. If the regulator cares much about consumers' surplus and little about the firm's profit, the L–M scheme may have undesirable distributive properties. Loeb and Magat did suggest that competitive bidding for the right to operate as a monopoly and receive the proposed subsidy could serve to return much of the surplus to consumers. We analyze this issue in more detail in Section 8.

The ability to observe the firm's expenditures can also help resolve these distributional issues. Sappington and Sibley (S–S) [77] proposed the following modification of Loeb and Magat's subsidy

---

[27] For details, see [74].

scheme. Suppose that in each period, the firm is afforded complete freedom over its pricing decisions. Also, in addition to retaining the profits from its activities in each period, the firm is given a subsidy equal to the *increment* in consumers' surplus that its output provides relative the level in the preceding period. The firm is also taxed an amount equal to the difference between revenues and expenditures in the previous period.

S–S show that under their regulatory scheme, the firm will produce at minimum cost and drop prices to the level of marginal cost immediately and not deviate from that position in subsequent periods. Consequently, at the price of a one-time subsidy to the firm, the regulator can ensure forever the outcome that maximizes total surplus even though he has no information whatsoever about the firm's technology.[28]

It is crucial for the implementation of the S–S regulatory scheme, like that of L–M, that the regulator and firm share the same information about the firm's demand function. Finsinger and Vogelsang (F–V) [29, 30] have proposed a related incentive scheme that is operational even when the regulator has no information about demand.[29] The scheme subsidizes the firm with an approximation to the increment in consumers' surplus called for under the S–S scheme. This approximation is given by $X(p_{t-1})[p_{t-1} - p_t]$. In terms of Figure 6.2, under the F–V scheme, the firm would be awarded a subsidy given by the area of rectangle A for reducing price from p_1 to p_2. The corresponding subsidy under the S–S scheme is the sum of the areas of regions A and B. Under both schemes the firm's accounting profits in the preceding period are taxed away in each period. F–V demonstrate that their scheme will induce the firm to minimize production costs and set prices that converge to marginal cost. Thus, though imperfect knowledge of demand will delay convergence to the regulator's most preferred outcome, this outcome can be implemented with the F–V scheme.

---

[28] S–S also show that the one-time subsidy to the firm can be eliminated if the firm's discount rate is known. They also demonstrate that their scheme will induce the firm to price at marginal cost and produce at minimum cost in a nonstationary environment.

[29] Finsinger and Vogelsang [29, 30] formally consider incentive plans for managers of public enterprises. Their basic insights are translated here to the case of regulated privately-held monopoly firms.

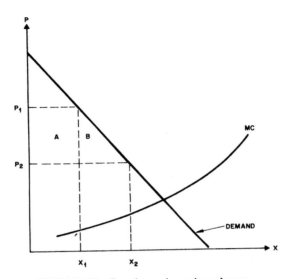

FIGURE 6.2   Regulatory incentive schemes.

The key conclusion of the literature, then, seems to be that the ability to observe the firm's expenditures repeatedly over a period of time can drastically mitigate the complications caused by problems of adverse selection. It is also the case that repeated interactions with observable past performance can resolve problems of moral hazard. Suppose that the regulated firm's decisions are made by a manager who is averse to effort. Radner [65] and Linhart, Radner, and Sinden [46] have shown that if the discount rate of the manager is sufficiently low and his personal costs from being dismissed are sufficiently great, the manager can be induced to act nearly in the regulator's interests without the imposition of undue risk.[30] The intuition commonly ascribed for this result is that with repeated interactions, the law of large numbers permits the regulator to more accurately distinguish between lack of diligence or effort by the firm and "bad luck" (that will be statistically offset by "good luck" over time). Consequently, the regulator is better able to motivate the desired behavior on the part of the firm. The

---

[30] See [64] for a precise statement of the result, along with additional intuition.

regulator may do so, for example, by threatening to terminate the management of the firm if performance over time is deemed sufficiently unsatisfactory.[31]

7. INTERTEMPORAL COMMITMENT

To this point, the models considered have presumed the regulator is able to commit himself to carry out the terms of any regulatory policy that is announced. This is indeed a powerful policy instrument for the regulator and one that may not be available in practice. For example, in the multiperiod Bayesian mechanism discussed in Section 6.1, the regulator commits to policies in future periods that are inefficient, given the information about the firm's costs that can be inferred from the firm's performance. In the extreme case where costs are the same in every period, the optimal regulatory policy has the regulator commit to establish a price in excess of marginal cost over the entire time horizon, even though the firm effectively reveals its actual production costs in the first period. If the current regulatory commission is unable to bind the actions of future regulatory commissions, it is unlikely that such a policy could be implemented, since future commissions would have an incentive to utilize the information revealed and to effect efficient prices.

The purpose of this section is to examine the implications of limited commitment ability on the part of the regulator. The focus of the chapter will be on the intertemporal Bayesian models discussed in Chapter 6. Section 7.1 discusses the commitment issue in the context of a binary model while Section 7.2 focuses on the case in which the firm's cost parameter can take on any one of a continuum of values. Section 7.3 concludes with a review of related work in the optimal taxation, planning, and procurement literature.

---

[31] A recent paper by Fudenberg et al. [32] suggests that these results should be attributed in part to the absence of a perfect capital market. In a principal-agent model with perfect capital markets and unlimited punishments, the authors find that under certain conditions, multiperiod interactions will not increase the ability of the principal to control the agent.

7.1. Commitment in a binary model

For simplicity we begin with a two-period, binary model in which the firm's cost function is linear; i.e.,

$$C(x, c_i) = c_i x + K, \qquad i \in \{L, H\},$$

and the marginal cost $c_i \in \{c_L, c_H\}$ is identical in each of the two periods. As shown in Section 6.1, the optimal Bayesian policy would have the regulator precommit to the following prices in both the first and second periods:

$$p_{tL} = c_L, \qquad\qquad\qquad\qquad t = 1, 2;$$
$$p_{tH} = c_H + \phi_L[2\beta - 1][\phi_H \beta]^{-1}[c_H - c_L] > c_H, \qquad t = 1, 2;$$

where all notation is as defined in the preceding sections. Thus, with probability ϕ_H, the higher marginal cost will be realized, and the regulator will establish a second-period price in excess of the level at which the firm's costs are known to be.

Suppose, now, that commitment across periods is not possible, and that in the second period the regulator will act to maximize his objective function given the information revealed in the first period. The optimal two-period policy with full commitment would not be feasible in this case, because the firm's choice of a price and tax in the first period reveals its costs with certainty. In the second period the regulator would implement the first-best policy of marginal cost pricing with a subsidy equal to fixed costs (i.e., $p_i = c_i$ and $T_i = -K$, for $i \in \{L, H\}$).

The regulator thus faces a choice. If he chooses a separating policy in period one (i.e., if the firm's true costs are perfectly identified by its actions in the first period), the firm recognizes that its profits will be zero in the second period. In order to induce the low-cost firm to reveal its superior capabilities, the regulator must increase the subsidy the firm is awarded for producing the larger output, $X(c_L)$. The additional subsidy compensates for the lower (zero) second-period profit the low-cost firm will receive when the regulator is unable to precommit to second-period profit levels. Alternatively, if the regulator chooses a pooling policy in the first period (i.e., the same price and tax for each type of firm), it learns nothing about the firm's true cost in the first period, and thus in the second period will implement the optimal single-period policy under asymmetric information.

Which of these two alternatives is preferred by the regulator depends upon the rights and duties of the regulated firm. Specifically, the choice depends upon whether the firm has the right to refuse to produce in the second period. Two cases are relevant here. In the first case, the firm must produce in the second period if the regulator allows it to earn a "fair" rate of return based on the costs "revealed" by the price-tax combination chosen in the first period. More precisely, if the firm implicitly claims to have costs c_j through its first-period activities, and if $\pi(p_{2j}, T_{2j}, c_j) \geq 0$ (where (p_{2j}, T_{2j}) is the second period price-tax combination for a firm that has revealed itself to have costs $c = c_j$), the firm is obligated to produce the assigned output, $X(p_{2j})$. This is analogous to a fair rate-of-return constraint, and will be referred to as the "fairness" case.

In the second case, the firm can refuse to produce in the second period with impunity. Thus, the firm will shut down whenever its *actual* profit is negative, even though its profit as calculated using its costs "revealed" in the first period might be positive. This second case affords the firm more freedom to misrepresent its private cost information; it corresponds to a situation of limited liability on the part of the firm, and will be referred to as the "limited liability" case. As will be seen, the equilibria may be quite different in these two cases.

7.1.1. *The "fairness" case.* In the fairness case, if the policy in period one is separating, the regulator will effect marginal cost pricing $(p_{2j} = c_j)$ in period two, and will subsidize fixed costs, K. Thus, separation in the first period leads to the first-best solution in the second period. On the other hand, if a pooling policy is implemented in period one, the regulator will have no new information at the start of period two, and thus will implement the optimal separating policy (described by Proposition 3.1) in period two. It turns out that the separating policy always leads to a higher expected surplus for the regulator.

PROPOSITION 7.1 *In the fairness case, the optimal first-period policy is a separating policy. Specifically:*

$$p_{1L} = c_L; \tag{7.1}$$

$$p_{1H} = c_H + \phi_L[2\beta - 1][\phi_H\beta]^{-1}[c_H - c_L]; \tag{7.2}$$

$$T_{1L} = -\{K + \bar{\pi} + [c_H - c_L][X(p_{1H}) + \delta X(c_H)]\}; \text{ and} \quad (7.3)$$

$$\pi(p_{1H}, T_{1H}; c_H) = \bar{\pi}, \quad (7.4)$$

where $\delta \in (0, 1]$ is the relevant discount rate for both the firm and the regulator.

The optimal first-period separating policy in the absence of commitment specifies prices that are equal to the optimal prices in a single-period model with adverse selection. A comparison of equations (7.3) and (3.3), however, reveals that the subsidy $(-T_{1L})$ for a firm with $c = c_L$ in the absence of commitment is greater than the corresponding subsidy in a single-period model.

A separating policy dominates a pooling policy in this regime for the following reason. Under a separating policy, the low-cost (c_L) firm enjoys an additional subsidy that is proportional to the additional profit $[c_H - c_L]X(c_H)$ it would earn in the second period if it "overstated" costs (i.e., it chose the price-tax combination (p_{1H}, T_{1H}) in the first period designed for a high-cost (c_H) firm). This additional profit would not be realized until the second period, however, so the extra subsidy needed to induce truthful revelation of costs, $\delta[c_H - c_L]X(c_H)$, is discounted. Thus, the "cost" associated with implementing the separating policy is discounted while some of the benefits of such a policy (i.e., the extra output from the low-cost producer) are realized in the first period. On the other hand, under the pooling policy, a deadweight loss occurs in the first period while the benefits from implementing the optimal single-period policy are not realized until the second period. Thus, costs are incurred immediately and the benefits delayed under the pooling policy. This difference in the timing of cost and benefit realizations is just sufficient to tip the balance in favor of implementing a separating policy in the first-period.

7.1.2. "Limited liability" case.

The limited liability restriction creates additional opportunities for strategic behavior for the firm that were not available in the "fairness" case. Consider a firm with high costs (c_H). Suppose that the firm "claimed" to have low costs (c_L) in the first period by choosing the price-tax combination (p_{1L}, T_{1L}). The possible attraction of understating costs is to acquire the relatively large subsidy that must be given to the low-cost producer to induce truthful cost revelation. The regulator would then infer that the firm has costs $c = c_L$ and establish a second-period policy that would eliminate all rents for this "low-cost" producer. However, under the limited liability regime, the firm can refuse to produce in the second period, thereby avoiding any losses. Thus, unlike the "fairness" case, there is a possibility in the limited liability case that the firm might actually want to *understate* costs to receive the larger subsidy awarded to the low-cost producer in the first period, and then refuse to produce in the second period. The next proposition indicates the consequences of this additional complication.

PROPOSITION 7.2 *In the limited liability regime:* (i) *If the discount factor δ is sufficiently small, the optimal first-period policy coincides with that of the fairness case.* (ii) *For higher values of δ, the optimal first-period policy may be fully separating or fully pooling. If it is fully separating, the optimal first-period policy is described by:*

$$p_{1L} < c_L. \tag{7.5}$$

$$p_{1H} > c_H + \phi_L[2\beta - 1][\phi_H\beta]^{-1}[c_H - c_L]. \tag{7.6}$$

$$T_{1L} = -\{K + \bar{\pi} + [c_H - c_L][X(p_{1H}) + \delta X(c_H)]\} + [p_{1L} - c_L]X(p_{1L}). \tag{7.7}$$

$$\pi(p_{1H}, T_{1H}; c_H) = \bar{\pi}. \tag{7.8}$$

Intuitively, if δ is very small, the gain to a high-cost firm from understating costs is relatively small because the subsidy to the low-cost producer $-T_{1L}$ is relatively small. This subsidy is equal to the discounted rents the low-cost firm could secure by exaggerating costs, and thus is smaller the smaller is δ. Consequently, the firm will have a reduced incentive to understate costs. Thus, when δ is small the binding incentive problem is to prevent cost exaggeration (as in the fairness regime), and the optimal policy in the limited liability regime will coincide with that in the fairness regime.

For higher values of δ, if the regulator attempts to implement a fully-separating policy a high-cost firm must be deterred from understating its costs in an attempt to collect the (relatively larger) subsidy designed for the low-cost producer. To accomplish this deterrence, the regulator must introduce two additional distortions.

First, a low-cost firm must be induced to charge a price below its marginal cost. Second, a high-cost firm must be induced to charge a price which exceeds the optimal single-period price when $c = c_H$. The first distortion increases output, and thus forces the high-cost producer who understates cost into a position of greater cost disadvantage. The second distortion reduces the subsidy $-T_{1L}$ to the low-cost firm (since that subsidy falls as the production level of the high-cost producer falls). Both distortions reduce the incentives to understate costs. Of course, the welfare loss that these additional distortions introduce may be sufficiently costly relative to the deadweight loss from pooling in the first period that this latter option is preferred. In general, the choice between a pooling policy and a separating policy in this case depends in a complex way on the discount rate, the differences in the firm's possible marginal costs, and the parameters of the demand function.

7.2. Commitment in a model with a continuum of possible cost realizations

With a continuum of possible cost realizations, the results of the analysis in the fairness case differ somewhat from the binary model. In particular, as Baron and Besanko [9] demonstrate, the regulator may find it optimal to induce some pooling in the first period. In the context of an example in which the demand curve is assumed to be linear and in which the regulator's prior beliefs are represented by a uniform distribution over $[c^-, c^+]$, Baron and Besanko show that it may be optimal to pool in the first period over an interval $[c_A, c^+]$ where $c_A \in (c^-, c^+)$. Full pooling ($c_A = c^-$) is never optimal which is consistent with the results in the binary case. The length of the pooling interval is a decreasing function of the discount factor, δ. Intuitively, this is sensible because the deadweight costs from pooling are incurred immediately while the benefits from pooling are delayed to the second period.

The difference between the binary case and the continuous case arises because with the continuous case it is more costly for the regulator to achieve a fully-separating equilibrium than it is in the binary case, since the regulator has less flexibility to discourage cost exaggeration in the continuous case. Under a fully-separating equilibrium with fairness, the firm must be given a reduction in tax relative to the full commitment case. By introducing some pooling in the first period the regulator is able to make this tax reduction less generous than it would otherwise have to be.

In the limited liability case, Baron and Besanko [9] and Laffont and Tirole [45] show in related models that when there is a continuum of possible cost realizations, a fully-separating equilibrium (i.e., an equilibrium in which a firm's technological capability is perfectly revealed in the first period) cannot arise.[32] This is in contrast to the binary case in which a fully-separating equilibrium is possible. The key feature of the binary setting which permits separation is the discrete difference in possible cost realizations. These discrete cost differences limit the range of cost misrepresentations the firm will attempt. To illustrate, in the binary case, if the low cost (c_L) is significantly less than the high cost (c_H), the high-cost firm will not wish to understate costs because the resulting price will be too far below its marginal cost. Consequently, the optimal regulatory policy need not be concerned with deterring cost understatement. By contrast, when there is a continuum of possible costs, these discrete differences disappear. Consequently, the firm can always misrepresent costs "slightly" with minimal deleterious effects on profits, so it becomes impossible for the regulator to induce a separating equilibrium.

With fully-separating equilibria in the first period ruled out, Laffont and Tirole [45] demonstrate that the equilibria may be quite complicated in general. However, if the regulator's initial uncertainty about the firm's cost is sufficiently small, the first-period contract will either be a full pooling contract or will exhibit pooling over a "large" subset of types. Intuitively, this occurs because with small uncertainty the deadweight loss from pooling in the first period is relatively small. Laffont and Tirole also derive necessary and sufficient conditions for a "partition equilibrium" to arise in the first period. A partition equilibrium is that in which the continuum of possible costs is partitioned into distinct intervals, and the firm receives the same first-period contract for all cost realizations in an interval.

---

[32] The model of Laffont and Tirole is actually a model of adverse selection and moral hazard in which realized costs are observable (as discussed in Section 5.1).

7.3. Related literature

The issue of intertemporal commitment has also been studied in a variety of other settings. These settings include: optimal taxation, automobile emissions regulation, central planning, and procurement. The commitment issue in the optimal taxation context is very similar to that in the regulatory context. The government does not know the ability of any particular worker in the economy, though it does know the distribution of abilities. The government's task is to design a tax schedule to maximize expected revenue. The schedule specifies taxes as a function of income. In a dynamic setting, the first-period income of a worker conveys information to the government about the worker's ability (which is the same in every period). In a model with full commitment, the government would commit to "ignore" this information; but it cannot do so when intertemporal commitment powers are absent. Two recent papers in the optimal tax literature have examined the implications of relaxing the commitment assumption. Roberts [71] has shown that in an infinite-horizon model with no discounting and no commitment, all workers will earn the same income and pay the same tax in each period. The rationale for this finding is quite intuitive. Whenever a worker reveals himself to have greater than the lowest ability, he forfeits forever the rents he could have gained from acting as if he had minimal ability. Thus, with no discounting of future utility, the cost to the government of achieving separation of worker of different abilities in any period is effectively infinite; so no separation will arise.

Of course, this finding follows from the extreme assumptions of no discounting and infinite lives. Brito *et al.* [8] present a finite horizon model and show that with a positive discount rate and a sufficiently long horizon, there will exist a period of time in which pooling occurs followed by a period of time in which a separating policy is followed. Note the correspondence here to the binary model with limited liability (of Section 7.2). In both settings, separation is optimal in the first period when the common discount factor is sufficiently small.

Yao [92] has studied the commitment issue in the context of a two-period model of automobile emissions regulation. Lacking the ability to precommit to future emission standards, the regulator adjusts second-period standards according to the firm's performance in meeting first-period requirements. A firm that demonstrates little difficulty in complying with the standard receives a more stringent standard in the second period than does a firm that exhibits significant compliance costs. This policy creates an incentive for the firm to underinvest in compliance in the first period in order to raise the observed costs of compliance and thereby reduce the stringency of second-period standards.

Yao's model is an example of the so-called "ratchet effect." The ratchet effect has been carefully studied in the central planning context in an important paper by Freixas *et al.* [31].[33] In their model, a firm has private information about its productivity. The planner learns about that productivity by observing the output produced by the firm. Recognizing this, the firm has an incentive to underproduce in order to convince the planner that its productivity is lower than it actually is, thereby increasing the reward for future output. The planner responds to this incentive by setting compensation for output in the first period above the level that would be optimal if full commitment were possible.[34]

The consequence of limited commitment in a procurement setting has been explored by Tirole [86]. Tirole presents a multiperiod model in which a purchaser possesses private information about a project's value while a supplier has private cost information. In the absence of commitment, the purchaser and supplier must bargain sequentially over whether to continue or cancel the project and over the payment for the project. One of Tirole's findings is that if the supplier must make an initial investment at the outset of the project, the level of that investment will generally be less than the investment the supplier would make if the purchaser and supplier could commit to a long-term contract.

Because the lack of commitment power generally entails welfare losses, it is clearly important to examine alternative forms of commitment. Anton and Yao [1] have presented a two-period

---

[33] The ratchet effect has also been studied in the context of the Soviet incentive model. See, for example, [42], [50], and [89].

[34] In an interesting paper, Lewis [48] has shown that the ratchet effect might be reversed if the planner can terminate a long-term project in the early stages of the project. In his model, the firm exerts extra effort in the early stages of the project in order to convince the planner that the project is worth undertaking.

procurement model in which the purchaser is presumed able to credibly commit to an auction in which the first-period supplier bids against potential alternative suppliers for the right to supply the product in the second period. The original supplier is assumed to benefit from an experience curve, and will therefore win the auction. He will also earn equilibrium rents in the second period equal to the difference between its costs and the costs of the most efficient alternative supplier. Thus, the first-period supplier knows that all rents will not be extracted in the second period. Consequently, in contrast to Laffont and Tirole [45], a fully-separating policy in the first period is possible.

8. INTER-FIRM COMPARISONS

To this point, the analysis has focused on the interaction between a regulator and a single firm. We have seen how the multiple observations afforded by repeated interactions can enable the regulator to better limit the firm's rents from private information. Another source of multiple observations for the regulator is comparison across firms. In settings where there is more than one regulated firm, the reports or actions of one firm can be compared to those of other firms. And where there is only a single incumbent firm initially, the regulator may find it advantageous to allow the entry of another firm. This is the case even when there are increasing returns to scale in the industry and the entrant's expected costs exceed those of the incumbent. The reduction in rents to the incumbent that a viable threat of entry secures can outweigh the losses that arise from the entrant's higher production costs.

There is another means by which the regulator may gain the benefits of competition among firms without having to incur duplicative or inefficient production technologies. This is accomplished via "franchise bidding," wherein firms bid for the right to serve as the sole producer of the regulated commodity. Depending upon the number of potential producers and their private information, franchise bidding can greatly enhance the regulator's ability to limit the rents of the monopoly producer.

In this section we explore each of these methods of control. Section 8.1 examines the optimal regulatory policy when there are multiple identical producers. Knowing (only) that firms are symmetric enables the regulator to ensure the most desired outcome with a particularly simple incentive scheme.

Section 8.2 briefly explores the optimal regulatory policy when the possibility of entry exists. Some parallels with the analysis of Section 4 are drawn, as the entrant's announced costs can be employed as an audit of the incumbent's costs. (The two cost parameters are assumed to be correlated.) However, because the entrant is also capable of production and because the entrant, like the incumbent, must be motivated to reveal its private cost information, important differences between the optimal auditing and entry policies arise.

Section 8.3 explores the optimal franchise bidding scheme. A key conclusion of the analysis is that it will generally be optimal for the regulator to introduce distortions at the production stage (i.e., induce the firm to produce an inefficiently small level of output) in order to foster more effective competition at the bidding stage.

8.1. Comparative performance of existing firms

In this section, we report on the findings of Nalebuff and Stiglitz [60] and Schleifer [79] to demonstrate the power of comparative performance. To begin, suppose that there are $n \geq 2$ firms each with the same technology, $C(x, c) = cx + R(c)$. $C(x, c)$ is the total cost of producing output x with marginal cost $c \in [c^-, c^+]$. $R(c)$ is the development expenditure required to achieve marginal production cost, c. It is assumed that $R(c^+) = 0$, $R'(c) < 0$ and $R''(c) > 0$. $\forall c \in [c^-, c^+]$. Thus, greater expenditures reduce operating costs, but at a decreasing rate.

The n firms in this setting might be thought of as local monopolies whose costs exhibit constant returns to scale in the relevant range. The first-best solution with n firms would have each price at marginal cost, earn zero profits, and undertake development to the point where the marginal benefits and costs are equated. Formally, letting p_i represent the price charged by firm i and T_i the associated tax on firm i $(i = 1, \ldots, n)$, we have:

DEFINITION 8.1 The first-best solution in this n-firm setting is given by:

  i) $T_i^* = -R(c^*),$ $i = 1, \ldots, n.$

  ii) $p_i^* = c^*,$ $i = 1, \ldots, n.$

  iii) $-R'(c^*) = x^* \equiv X(p_i^*).$

Now, suppose that the regulator has no knowledge of the identical demand curve facing each firm or of the $R(\cdot)$ function, but can observe realized production costs and development expenditures. It turns out that this latter information is sufficient to achieve the social optimum in this "symmetric environment".[35]

PROPOSITION 8.1 *When the regulator sets $p_i = \{\sum_{j \neq i} c_j\}[n - 1]^{-1}$ and $T_i = -\{\sum_{j \neq i} R(c_j)\}[n - 1]^{-1} \; \forall \, i = 1, \ldots, n$, the unique Nash equilibrium in this symmetric environment is for each firm to pick $c_i = c^*$.*

In other words, when each firm is required to set its price equal to the average operating cost of all other firms and is compensated for its development costs at the average level of expenditures of other firms, the proper incentives are created for cost minimization. The key point is that a firm's compensation does not depend upon its own performance. And, with price established at c^* (in equilibrium), no firm will find it advantageous to select a cost level higher than c^*, since the associated marginal savings $(R'(c))$ are outweighed by the increment in production costs $(x(c)) \; \forall \, c > c^*$. Similarly, there will be no incentive to select a lower cost level.

When firms differ according to immutable observable characteristics, the incentive scheme described above can be readily modified to effect the "handicapping" necessary to ensure the social optimum. When firms differ in ways that are not readily observed by the regulator, however, it will generally not be possible to implement the social optimum, as is noted in Sections 8.2 and 8.3. Thus, the presumed symmetry of firms is quite a strong assumption.

8.2. Designing entry policy

In preceding sections, we have examined how the regulator can set prices, structure taxes, and conduct audits to limit the rents that

---

[35] The details of the proof of Proposition 8.1 can be found in [79].

accrue to a privately informed incumbent monopolist. In this section, we briefly consider an additional policy instrument that may be available to the regulator—allowing entry by a second producer. This policy instrument can be of value to the regulator when the production costs of the incumbent and potential entrant are correlated.

When costs are correlated, the entrant's cost report can serve as an audit of the incumbent's report, much along the lines discussed in Section 4. With sunk costs of production and increasing returns to scale, promoting entry to limit the incumbent's rents is not without cost. Nevertheless, entry may still be optimal, particularly when the assets the entrant must sink to learn its operating costs are relatively small.

A key difference between models of entry and auditing is that in the former, the monitor is subject to moral hazard. In other words, when the relevant information about an incumbent's costs is observed privately by a new entrant rather than being publicly observed, truthful reporting of the information must be induced, generally at some social cost. An additional difference between the classes of models is that with entry, the "monitor" is capable of production. Thus, if the monitor turns out to have lower operating costs than the incumbent, the former may replace the latter in the industry. In fact, it is also possible that an incumbent will be optimally replaced by an entrant though the entrant is known to have *higher* costs than the incumbent.[36] The reason is that the added discipline this policy places on the incumbent can outweigh the expected losses from productive inefficiency.

Other differences between optimal entry and auditing policies also arise. For example, entry may be admitted more or less often than auditing occurs, *ceteris paribus*. Because entry carries with it the possibility of lower production costs, it is generally a more valuable policy instrument for the regulator. Thus it may be used more intensively. On the other hand, because the threat of entry (and possible shutdown of the incumbent) provides a more effective deterrent against cost exaggeration by the incumbent, actual entry

---

[36] See [25] for a proof of this result as well as additional explanation. For related work on the economics of incentive compatible contracts with multiple agents, see [23].

may not have to be allowed as often. For related reasons, industry prices may well be higher or lower following entry than following an audit—even if the entrant does not actually produce any output.[37]

The key point is that although entry can serve a role much like auditing, its distinct features can result in subtle variations in the regulator's use of this and other policy instruments.

8.3. Franchise bidding

We turn now to consider the situation in which it is prohibitively costly for more than one firm to incur the fixed (sunk) costs of production. Consequently, the regulator will allow only one firm to produce in the industry. However, when there is more than one potential producer, competition for the right to produce can limit the rents of the monopolist. This idea dates back at least to Demsetz [22], who argued the merits of franchise bidding. Loeb and Magat (L–M) [51] proposed a particular franchise bidding scheme whereby the chosen monopolist is awarded a subsidy equal to the level of consumers' surplus generated by the price he charges for his output.[38] This scheme induces the firm to equate price and marginal cost. Further, with "sufficient competition" among potential producers, the rents of the monopolist can be eliminated. Note that the (L–M) scheme requires only that the regulator know the demand curve facing the producer; he need share none of the potential producers' cost information.

Should the regulator have some knowledge of possible cost structures, however, this knowledge can be used to improve upon the clever L–M bidding scheme.[39] More specifically, suppose that the production technology is known to be characterized by the linear cost function $C(x, c) = cx + K$, with $c \in [c^-, c^+]$, and K representing a large fixed cost that must be sunk by any producer before marginal production cost, c, is known with certainty. Further, suppose that prior to bidding for the right to operate the franchise, each of the n potential producers acquires an indepen-

---

[37] Again, see [25] for details. For related work, see [19] and [1].

[38] The scheme is analogous to the "complete decentralization" schemes discussed by [37], [41], and [80]. See also [40].

[39] The following discussion is based on the model presented in [68].

dent assessment, v_i, of his likely marginal production cost. Formally, these assessments can be modeled as independent draws from a uniform distribution on the interval $[0, 1]$. Higher v draws signal that lower production costs are more likely in the sense of first-order stochastic dominance, so the "valuation" of the franchise is greater. Thus, letting $F(c \mid v)$ be the distribution function for c conditional on v, we have $F_v(c \mid v) \geq 0 \; \forall \, c \in [c^-, c^+], \; v \in [0, 1]$, where the subscript indicates the relevant partial derivative.

The timing under consideration is the following. First, each of the n potential producers privately learns v_i. Then, the regulator announces the terms of the bidding procedure. Next, the highest bidder is awarded the sole right to produce the commodity in question. This producer then sinks the fixed costs, K, and privately observes marginal cost, c. He then decides how much to produce, and is compensated as initially promised by the regulator.

In this setting, with both K and the functional forms of $C(\cdot)$ and $F(\cdot)$ common knowledge throughout, the regulator can generally achieve a higher level of expected net consumers' surplus than the level secured by the L–M bidding scheme. Intuitively, the reason is that the L–M scheme offers the same *ex post* compensation schedule (equal to sum of realized profit and consumers' surplus for any output level) to each producer, regardless of his bid. But by tying the compensation schedule to the winning bid, self-selection of informed bidders is effected which limits the rents to the selected producer.

This critical "linkage" between the bidding and production stages is accomplished by what Riordan and Sappington [68] refer to as "menu contracting." [40] The regulator designs a menu of rank-ordered compensation schedules: one is associated with each possible bid. The producer that agrees to produce under the terms of the most highly ranked schedule is awarded the franchise. The menu of contracts is designed to limit the incentives of bidders to underbid (i.e., exaggerate prospective costs by understating v_i). This is accomplished by associating with lower bids compensation schedules under which payments to the firm rise less rapidly with output than does consumers' surplus. The effect is to reduce

---

[40] For a detailed discussion of the "linkage effect" on bidding models, see [56] and [57]. Menu bidding has also been examined in [15].

production levels below first-best levels (i.e., those that would result
if there were no information asymmetry). In particular, optimal
output levels $x(c, v)$ as a function of v and c are given by:[41]

$$V'(x(c, v)) = c + [1 - v]F_v(c \mid v)[F_c(c \mid v)]^{-1} \geq c, \qquad (8.1)$$

where $V(\cdot)$ represents consumers' surplus. Output distortions are
generally greater the lower is the bid. These distortions limit the
expected rents of the producer, and by a greater amount the higher
is v_i. This differential effect is what reduces the incentives of firms
to shade their bids, and thus secures greater rents for consumers.

Another important feature of the optimal incentive scheme in this
setting is that for any given bid and cost realization pair, output
distortions are independent of the number of bidders. (This fact is
apparent from equation (8.1).) Thus, there is a clear distinction
between the screening function of the auction, and the rent-
extraction function of the compensation schedule. This conclusion
stems from two offsetting effects as the number of bidders increases.
First, greater competition for the franchise makes potential producers bid more aggressively, which reduces the need for (costly)
output distortions. Second, with a greater number of bidders, the
expected return from any output distortion (in terms of the
associated reduction in rents for bidders with more favorable
valuations of the franchise) increases. With independent private
valuations of the franchise, the second effect exactly offsets the first,
and the stated independence result arises. Even though output
levels are independent of the number of bidders, the winning firm's
compensation does depend on the number of bidders. Specifically,
the "franchise fee" that must be paid by the winner of the auction is
an increasing function of the number of bidders. Intuitively, with a
larger number of bidders, potential producers bid more aggressively, and the regulatory authority can exploit this aggressive
behavior by imposing a higher "tax" on the winner of the auction.

Similar results are derived in bidding models that incorporate

---

[41] Note the first-best quantity levels will be effected for $v = 1$ and whenever
$F_v(c, v) = 0$; in particular, for $c = c^-$ and $c = c^+$. Further note that the induced
quantity levels for any (c, v) pair is independent of the number of bidders.

both moral hazard and adverse selection considerations. (See [44], [52] and [55]). In these models, potential producers are perfectly informed from the outset about the (stochastic) relationships between their subsequent productive effort and output. More able producers know that their effort is more likely to result in greater output (in the sense of stochastic dominance). Under the assumption that greater effort at the production stage can exactly compensate for innate ability deficiencies, the menu of contracts that is optimally offered to potential producers will consist entirely of compensation schedules that are linear in output, provided certain regularity conditions are satisfied.[42] Schedules that promise a larger fraction of the (value of) output to the producer require a larger lump-sum payment by the producer. More able (risk-neutral) producers will be willing to pay the larger up-front fee, knowing that they are likely to produce large amounts of output.[43]

The key point, again, is that the terms of compensation for production vary systematically according to the winning bid. Though productive inefficiencies are introduced by doing so, the gains that arise from more competitive bidding outweigh these losses. Thus, although competition at one stage of activity (i.e., bidding) can substitute for competition at another stage (production), the two stages generally remain linked in important respects.

---

[42] This is the finding of McAfee and McMillan [52]. In a slightly different setting, Laffont and Tirole [44] derive optimal compensation schedules that are linear in the observed cost statistic. McAfee and McMillan [54] derive related conclusions in a setting where output is produced by a team, rather than by a single producer.

[43] Riordan and Sappington [68] extend their analysis to incorporate limits on the size of franchise fees that can be collected from producers. (Such limits are of practical importance when the initial wealth of producers is small relative to the expected surplus from production, and when capital markets are imperfect.) They find that similar production distortions characterize the optimal incentive scheme in this setting. The authors also consider the possibility that the regulator cannot credibly commit to the terms of a production contract at the time bidding takes place. Thus, any information about the winning bidder's valuation that is inferred from his bid will be used by the regulator to limit the producer's rents when designing the production contract. Even in the absence of intertemporal commitment abilities, the regulator may induce an equilibrium at the bidding stage that is completely separating, so that the producer's valuation can be inferred perfectly from his bid.

9. EXTENSIONS AND FUTURE DIRECTIONS

In this concluding section, we point out some questions that remain unanswered in the literature. We also outline the directions in which research is proceeding.

As complex as some of the formal models in this literature are, the problems considered pale in comparison to those that must be solved before our understanding of and prescriptions for regulatory policy are close to complete. One reason for this conclusion is the manner in which the regulator's knowledge is depicted in formal models. Though Bayesian formulations with a single unknown technological parameter do allow one to write down tractable problems that reflect limited information, they also presume substantial knowledge on the part of the regulator. Knowing the functional form of the firm's cost function, the probability structures, and the complete set of all possible contingencies constitutes a great deal of information. In practice, regulators' information is unlikely to be so expansive; thus, communication and contracting with the firm will be more problematic than is generally depicted in these Bayesian formulations.

As noted in Section 6, an extreme alternative to such formulations is to presume the regulator has no knowledge of some aspects of the regulatory environment. Some insight is certainly gained from this alternative, but a middle ground would seem more appropriate.[44] One obvious possibility is to incorporate multidimensional uncertainty in Bayesian formulations. The mathematical complexity introduced by doing so, however, presents formidable problems.[45]

It also seems important that regulatory matters be viewed from a broader perspective. Most models in the literature focus exclusively on the interaction between the regulator (who is endowed with the Stackelberg leader role) and the firm (in the role of follower).[46]

---

[44] Grossman and Hart [35] suggest a promising modeling technique, whereby certain contingencies cannot be contracted upon, though they may be foreseen by all parties. Dye [27] suggests an approach wherein the costs of writing more complete contracts are explicitly considered. Of course, all of these studies are an outgrowth of Williamson's [91] pioneering work on transactions costs.

[45] For interesting analyses along these lines, see [72] and [53].

[46] An exception is Spulber [82], who views the regulator as an arbitrator in a bargaining game between consumers and the firm, where each party has relevant private information.

Further, most studies presume that the regulator acts benevolently in the social interest. In practice, the relationship between regulator and regulated firm is but one link in a hierarchical chain of relationships; and the regulator may be better viewed as a self-interested agent of Congress or consumers as well as a "principal" to the regulated firm.[47] Furthermore, it must be recognized (as in [5]) that there are often multiple regulators in charge of overseeing various aspects of a particular firm's activities. And when the mandates and interests of the regulators are not entirely coincidental, important complications to the "standard" analysis are introduced.

The question of regulatory mandates emphasizes the fact that specification of appropriate regulatory boundaries is a nontrivial exercise. The very question of whether certain (or all) of a firm's activities should be regulated or unregulated is often a difficult one. And when it has been decided that regulation of some activities is no longer appropriate, managing the transition to deregulation can be quite complicated. Careful study of these issues seems warranted.

Another direction in which these regulatory models could be profitably pursued concerns the problems of monitoring the performance of the regulated firm. In practice, there are many dimensions of the firm's performance, including the quality of the product, as well as the quantity produced and its cost. Designing incentive schemes when the commodity is multifaceted and difficult to observe precisely can be a formidable task.[48]

To put these calls for additional research in perspective, we close with a thought raised at the outset. This *is* a relatively new field of research, and much has been learned in the past few years. It seems safe to predict that we will know much more a few years hence.

References

[1] Anton, J. J. and D. A. Yao: "Second-Sourcing and the Experience Curve: Price Competition in Defense Procurement," *Rand Journal of Economics* (forthcoming).

---

[47] For a formal analysis along those lines, see [24]. A related model is that of Lewis [49].

[48] Some thoughts along these lines are developed in [34] and [85].

[2] Averch, H. and L. L. Johnson, "Behavior of the Firm Under Regulatory Constraint," *American Economic Review*, **52** (1962), 1052–1069.

[3] Baron, D. P., "Price Regulation, Product Quality, and Asymmetric Information," *American Economic Review*, **71** (1981), 212–220.

[4] Baron, D. P., "Regulatory Strategies Under Asymmetric Information," in *Bayesian Models in Economic Theory*, ed. by M. Boyer and R. Kihlstrom, 155–180. Amsterdam: North-Holland, 1984.

[5] Baron, D. P., "Noncooperative Regulation of a Nonlocalized Externality," *Rand Journal of Economics*, **16** (1985), 553–568.

[6] Baron, D. P., "Optimal Regulatory Mechanism Design," in *Handbook of Industrial Organization*, ed. by R. Schmalensee and R. Willig. Amsterdam: North Holland (forthcoming).

[7] Baron, D. P. and D. Besanko, "Regulation, Asymmetric Information, and Auditing," *Rand Journal of Economics*, **15** (1984), 447–470.

[8] Baron, D. P. and D. Besanko, "Regulation and Information in a Continuing Relationship," *Information Economics and Policy*, **1** (1984), 267–302.

[9] Baron, D. P. and D. Besanko, "Commitment and Fairness in a Dynamic Regulatory Relationship," *Review of Economic Studies* (forthcoming).

[10] Baron, D. P. and D. Besanko, "Monitoring, Moral Hazard, Asymmetric Information, and Risk Sharing in Procurement Contracting," Research Paper No. 832R, Stanford Graduate School of Business (1986).

[11] Baron, D. P. and R. R. Debondt, "On the Design of Regulatory Price Adjustment Mechanisms," *Journal of Economic Theory*, **24** (1981), 70–94.

[12] Baron, D. P. and R. B. Myerson, "Regulating a Monopolist with Unknown Costs," *Econometrica*, **50** (1982), 911–930.

[13] Baumol, W. J. and D. Bradford, "Optimal Departures from Marginal Cost Pricing," *American Economic Review*, **67** (1970), 265–283.

[14] Baumol, W. J. and A. K. Klevorick, "Input Choice and Rate-of-Return Regulation: An Overview of the Discussion," *Bell Journal of Economics and Management Science*, **1** (1970), 162–190.

[15] Bernheim, B. D. and M. D. Whinston, "Menu Auctions, Resource Allocation, and Economic Influence," *Quarterly Journal of Economics*, **101** (1986), 1–32.

[16] Besanko, D., "On the Use of Revenue Requirements Regulation Under Imperfect Information," in *Analyzing the Impact of Regulatory Change in Public Utilities*, ed. by M. A. Crew, 39–55. Lexington, MA: Lexington Books, 1985.

[17] Besanko, D. and D. S. Sibley, "Delegation and Transfer Pricing in a Principal-Agent Model," Economics Discussion Paper, Bell Communications Research, Inc., (1986).

[18] Brito, R., J. Hamilton, S. Slutsky, and J. E. Stiglitz, "Taxation and Commitment," unpublished working paper, (1985).

[19] Caillaud, B., "Regulation, Competition, and Asymmetric Information," unpublished paper, Massachusetts Institute of Technology, (1986).

[20] Caillaud, B., R. Guesnerie, P. Rey, and J. Tirole, "The Normative Economics of Government Intervention in Production," Technical Report 473, Institute for Mathematical Studies in the Social Sciences, Stanford University, (1985).

[21] Dasgupta, P. S., P. J. Hammond, and E. S. Maskin, "The Implementation of Social Choice Rules: Some Results on Incentive Compatibility," *Review of Economic Studies*, **46** (1979), 185–216.

[22] Demsetz, H., "Why Regulate Utilities?" *Journal of Law and Economics*, **7** (1968), 55–65.

[23] Demski, J. S. and D. E. M. Sappington, "Optimal Incentive Contracts with Multiple Agents," *Journal of Economic Theory*, **33** (1984), 152–171.

[24] Demski, J. S. and D. E. M. Sappington, "Hierarchical Regulatory Control," Economics Discussion Paper, Bell Communications Research, Inc., (1986).

[25] Demski, J. S., D. E. M. Sappington and P. T. Spiller, "Managing Supplier Switching," *Rand Journal of Economics*, (1987, forthcoming).

[26] Dupuit, J., "On the Measurement of the Utility of Public Works," *International Economics Papers*, Vol. 2, (1952), 83–110 (translated by R. H. Barback from "de la Mesure de l'Utilité des Travaux Publics," *Annals des Ponts et Chausées*, 2nd Series, Vol. 8, (1944)).

[27] Dye, R., "Costly Contract Contingencies," *International Economic Review*, **26** (1985), 223–250.

[28] Faulhaber, G. R., "Cross-Subsidization: Pricing in Public Enterprises," *American Economic Review*, **61** (1975), 966–977.

[29] Finsinger, J. and I. Vogelsang, "Alternative Institutional Frameworks for Price Incentive Mechanisms," *Kyklos*, **34** (1981), 388–404.

[30] Finsinger, J. and I. Vogelsang, "Strategic Management Behavior Under Reward Structures in a Planned Economy," *Quarterly Journal of Economics*, **100** (1985), 263–270.

[31] Freixas, X., R. Guesnerie, and J. Tirole, "Planning under Incomplete Information and the Ratchet Effect," *Review of Economic Studies*, **52** (1985), 85–95.

[32] Fudenberg, D., B. Holmstrom, and P. Milgrom, "Repeated Moral Hazard with Borrowing and Saving," unpublished working paper, Yale University, (1986).

[33] Goldman, M. B., H. E. Leland, and D. S. Sibley, "Optimal Nonuniform Prices," *Review of Economic Studies*, **51** (1984), 305–319.

[34] Gravelle, H. S. E., "Reward Structures in a Planned Economy: Some Difficulties," *Quarterly Journal of Economics*, **100** (1985), 271–278.

[35] Grossman, S. J. and O. D. Hart, "The Costs and Benefits of Ownership: A Theory of Vertical and Lateral Integration," *Journal of Political Economy*, **94** (1986), 691–719.

[36] Guesnerie, R. and J.-J. Laffont, "A Complete Solution to a Class of Principal-Agent Problems with an Application to the Control of a Self-Managed Firm," *Journal of Public Economics*, **25** (1984), 329–369.

[37] Harris, M. and A. Raviv, "Some Results on Incentive Contracts with Applications to Education and Employment, Health Insurance, and Law Enforcement," *American Economic Review*, **68** (1978), 20–30.

[38] Harris, M. and A. Raviv, "Optimal Incentive Contracts with Imperfect Information," *Journal of Economic Theory*, **20** (1979), 231–259.

[39] Harris, M. and R. M. Townsend, "Resource Allocation Under Asymmetric Information," *Econometrica*, **49** (1981), 33–64.

[40] Hildenbrant, G., "Optimal Subsidy Functions," United States Air Force mimeo, (1977).

[41] Holmstrom, B., "On Incentives and Control in Organizations," *Bell Journal of Economics*, **10** (1979), 74–91.

[42] Holmstrom, B., "Design of Incentive Schemes and the New Soviet Incentive Model," *European Economic Review*, **26** (1982), 127–148.

[43] Hotelling, H., "The General Welfare in Relation to Problems of Taxation and of Railway and Utility Rates," *Econometrica*, **6** (1938), 242–269.

[44] Laffont, J.-J. and J. Tirole: "Using Cost Observation to Regulate Firms," *Journal of Political Economy*, **94** (1986), 614–641.

[45] Laffont, J.-J. and J. Tirole: "The Dynamics of Incentive Contracts," unpublished working paper, Massachusetts Institute of Technology, (1986).

[46] Linhart, P., R. Radner, and F. Sinden, "A Sequential Principal-Agent Approach to Regulation," Bell Laboratories Discussion Paper, (1983).

[47] Lee, W. and A. V. Thakor, "Optimal Regulatory Pricing and Capital Investment Under Asymmetric Information About Cost," *Southern Economic Journal* (forthcoming).

[48] Lewis, T. R., "Reputation and Contractual Performance in Long-Term Projects," *Rand Journal of Economics,* **17** (1986), 141–157.

[49] Lewis, T. R., "Budget Competition in Project Funding," unpublished working paper, University of California at Davis, (1986).

[50] Loeb, M. and W. Magat, "Success Indicators in the Soviet Union: The Problem of Incentives and Efficient Allocations," *American Economic Review,* **68** (1978), 173–181.

[51] Loeb, M. and W. Magat, "A Decentralized Method for Utility Regulation," *Journal of Law and Economics,* **22** (1979), 399–404.

[52] McAfee, R. P. and J. McMillan, "Bidding for Contracts: A Principal-Agent Analysis," *Rand Journal of Economics,* **17** (1986), 326–350.

[53] McAfee, R. P. and J. McMillan, "Multidimensional Incentive Compatibility and Mechanism Design," unpublished working paper, University of Western Ontario, (1986).

[54] McAfee, R. P. and J. McMillan, "Optimal Contracts for Teams," unpublished working paper, University of Western Ontario, (1986).

[55] McAfee, R. P. and J. McMillan, "Competition for Agency Contracts," Technical Report No. 10, Centre for Decision Sciences and Econometrics, University of Western Ontario, (1986).

[56] Milgrom, P., "Auction Theory," unpublished working paper, Yale University, (1985).

[57] Milgrom, P. and R. Weber, "A Theory of Auctions and Competitive Bidding," *Econometrica,* **50** (1982), 1089–1122.

[58] Mirrlees, J., "An Exploration in the Theory of Optimum Income Taxation," *Review of Economic Studies,* **38** (1971), 175–208.

[59] Myerson, R. B., "Incentive Compatibility and the Bargaining Problem," *Econometrica,* **47** (1979), 61–74.

[60] Nalebuff, B. and J. E. Stiglitz, "Information, Competition and Markets," *American Economic Review,* **14** (1983), 278–283.

[61] Panzar. J. C., "A Neoclassical Approach to Peak Load Pricing," *Bell Journal of Economics,* **7** (1976), 521–530.

[62] Panzar, J. C. and R. D. Willig, "Free Entry and the Sustainability of Natural Monopoly," *Bell Journal of Economics,* **8** (1977), 1–22.

[63] Polinsky, A. and S. Shavell, "The Optimal Tradeoff Between the Probability and Magnitude of Fines," *American Economic Review,* **69** (1979), 880–891.

[64] Radner, R., "Monitoring Cooperative Agreements in a Repeated Principal-Agent Relationship," *Econometrica,* **49** (1981), 1127–1148.

[65] Radner, R., "Repeated Moral Hazard with Low Discount Rates," Bell Laboratories Discussion Paper, (1984).

[66] Ramsey, F., "A Contribution to the Theory of Taxation," *Economic Journal,* **37** (1927), 47–61.

[67] Riordan, M. H., "On Delegating Price Authority to a Regulated Firm," *Rand Journal of Economics,* **15** (1984), 108–115.

[68] Riordan, M. H. and D. E. M. Sappington, "Awarding Monopoly Franchises," *American Economic Review* (forthcoming).

[69] Riordan, M. H. and D. E. M. Sappington, "Designing Procurement Contracts," Economics Discussion Paper, Bell Communications Research, Inc., (1986).

[70] Roberts, K. W. S., "Welfare Implications of Nonlinear Prices," *Economic Journal*, **89** (1979), 66–83.

[71] Roberts, K. W. S., "The Theoretical Limits to Redistribution," *Review of Economic Studies*, **51** (1984), 177–195.

[72] Rochet, J. C., "Monopoly Regulation With Two-Dimensional Uncertainty," unpublished working paper, (1984).

[73] Ross, S. A., "The Economic Theory of Agency: The Principal's Problem," *American Economic Review*, **63** (1973), 134–139.

[74] Sappington, D. E. M., "Strategic Firm Behavior Under a Dynamic Regulatory Adjustment Process," *The Bell Journal of Economics*, **11** (1980), 360–372.

[75] Sappington, D. E. M., "Optimal Regulation of a Multiproduct Monopoly With Unknown Technological Capabilities," *Bell Journal of Economics*, **14** (1983), 453–463.

[76] Sappington, D. E. M., "Commitment to Regulatory Bureaucracy," *Information Economics and Policy*, (forthcoming).

[77] Sappington, D. E. M. and D. S. Sibley, "Regulatory Incentive Schemes Using Historic Cost Data," Economics Discussion Paper, Bell Communications Research, Inc., (1985).

[78] Sappington, D. E. M. and J. E. Stiglitz, in E. Bailey (ed.), *Public Regulation: New Perspectives on Institutions and Policies*. Cambridge: The MIT Press (forthcoming).

[79] Schleifer, A., "A Theory of Yardstick Competition," *Rand Journal of Economics*, **16** (1985), 319–327.

[80] Shavell, S., "Risk Sharing and Incentives in the Principal and Agent Relationship," *Bell Journal of Economics*, **10** (1979), 55–73.

[81] Spence, A. M., "Nonlinear Prices and Welfare," *Journal of Public Economics*, **8** (1977), 1–18.

[82] Spulber, D. F., "Bargaining and Regulation with Asymmetric Information about Demand and Supply," *Journal of Economic Theory* (forthcoming).

[83] Steiner, P. O., "Peak Loads and Efficient Pricing," *Quarterly Journal of Economics*, **71** (1957), 585–610.

[84] Stiglitz, J. E., "Risk Sharing and Incentives in Sharecropping," *Review of Economic Studies*, **41** (1974), 219–256.

[85] Tam, M., "Reward Structures in a Planned Economy: Some Further Thoughts," *Quarterly Journal of Economics*, **50** (1985), 279–290.

[86] Tirole, J., "Procurement and Renegotiation," *Journal of Political Economy*, **94** (1986), 235–259.

[87] Townsend, R., "Optimal Multiperiod Contracts and the Gain from Enduring Relationships Under Private Information," *Journal of Political Economy*, **90** (1982), 1166–1186.

[88] Vogelsang, I. and J. Finsinger, "A Regulatory Adjustment Process for Optimal Pricing by Multiproduct Monopoly Firms," *Bell Journal of Economics*, **10** (1979), 157–171.

[89] Weitzman, M. L., "The Ratchet Principle and Performance Incentives," *Bell Journal of Economics*, **11** (1980), 302–308.

[90] Williamson, O. E., "Peak Load Pricing and Optimal Capacity Under Indivisibility Constraints," *American Economic Review,* **56** (1966), 810–827.
[91] Williamson, O. E., *Markets and Hierarchies.* New York: The Free Press. 1975.
[92] Yao, D. A., "Strategic Responses to Automobile Emissions Control: A Game-Theoretic Approach," unpublished working paper, University of Pennsylvania, (1986).

Appendix to Section 3

Proof of Lemma 3.1

As a first step we demonstrate that (3.6) and (3.7) are equivalent to (3.10) and (3.12). Then, the "transformed" objective function will be derived. Throughout the proof of this lemma we will work with the output schedule, $x(c)$, where $x(c) = X(p(c))$.

(a) Proof that (3.6) and (3.7) are equivalent to (3.10) and (3.12).

First we prove that (3.7) implies (3.10) and (3.12). Define:

$$\pi(c) \equiv \pi(p(c), T(c); c).$$

Using the definition of $\pi(p, T; c)$, (3.7) implies that

$$\pi(c) - \pi(\hat{c}) \geq C(x(\hat{c}), \hat{c}) - C(x(\hat{c}), c). \tag{A3.1}$$

Similarly, it follows that:

$$\pi(\hat{c}) - \pi(c) \geq C(x(c), c) - C(x(c), \hat{c}). \tag{A3.2}$$

Combining (A3.1) and (A3.2) yields:

$$C(x(c), \hat{c}) - C(x(c), c) \geq \pi(c) - \pi(\hat{c})$$
$$\geq C(x(\hat{c}), \hat{c}) - C(x(\hat{c}), c). \tag{A3.3}$$

Recall that Assumption 3.8 stated that $C_{xc} > 0$. Using this assumption, (A3.3) can be shown to imply that $x(c) \geq x(\hat{c})$ when $\hat{c} > c$. Thus (3.12) is proven. To prove (3.7), assume that $\hat{c} > c$, and divide each side of (A3.3) by $\hat{c} - c$. Then, taking limits as $\hat{c}$ approaches c, one obtains:

$$\pi'(c) = -C_c(x(c), c). \tag{A3.4}$$

Integrating (A3.4) yields:

$$\pi(c) = \int_c^{\bar{c}} C_c(x(t), t)\, dt + \pi(\bar{c}). \tag{A3.5}$$

Now, the individual rationality constraint (3.6) requires that $\pi(c)$ be at least as large as $\bar{\pi}$ for each $c \in [c^-, \bar{c}]$. From (A3.4) $\pi(c)$ is strictly decreasing in c, so the individual rationality constraint is optimally satisfied by setting $\pi(\bar{c}) = \bar{\pi}$. Then (A3.5) can be rewritten as:

$$\pi(c) = \int_c^{\bar{c}} C_c(x(t), t)\, dt + \bar{\pi}. \tag{A3.6}$$

As a final step in this part of the proof, use the definition of $\pi(c)$ in conjunction with (A3.5) to obtain:

$$P(x(c))x(c) - C(x(c), c) - T(c) = \int_c^{\bar{c}} C(x(t), t)\, dt + \bar{\pi}. \tag{A3.7}$$

Rearranging (A3.7) yields (3.10).

We now prove that (3.10) and (3.12) imply (3.6) and (3.7). Note that (3.10) immediately implies (A3.6) which, in turn, implies that $\pi(c) \geq \bar{\pi}$ for every $c \in [c^-, \bar{c}]$.

To prove (3.7) note that

$$\pi(c) - \pi(p(\hat{c}), T(\hat{c}); c) = \pi(c) - \pi(\hat{c})$$
$$- [C(x(\hat{c}), \hat{c}) - C(x(\hat{c}), c)]. \tag{A3.8}$$

Using (3.6), (A3.8) can be rewritten as follows:

$$\pi(c) - \pi(p(\hat{c}), T(\hat{c}); c) = \int_c^{\hat{c}} C_c(x(t), t)\, dt$$
$$- [C(x(\hat{c}), \hat{c}) - C(x(\hat{c}), c)],$$
$$= \int_c^{\hat{c}} \{C_c(x(t), t) - C_c(x(\hat{c}), t)\}\, dt. \tag{A3.9}$$

Now, suppose $\hat{c} > c$. Assumption 3.8 in conjunction with (3.12) implies that the integral on the right-side of (A3.9) is positive. If $\hat{c} < c$, Assumption 3.8 and (3.12) imply that the integrand is negative. However, the order of integration is reversed, so the integral is positive. Thus

$$\pi(c) - \pi(p(\hat{c}), T(\hat{c}); c) \geq 0,$$

proving (3.7).

(b) Derivation of the "transformed" objective function.

As a first step, note that there is no loss of generality if all terms in the objective function for problem [RP-C] are divided by the positive constant β. Next, from the definition of $\pi(p, T; c)$ and from the fact that $S(p) = V(x) - P(x)x$ it is easily verified that

$$\int_{c^-}^{\bar{c}} \{S(p(c)) + T(c) + [1 - \beta]\beta^{-1}[\pi(p(c), T(c); c) - \bar{\pi}]\}f(c)\, dc$$

$$= \int_{c^-}^{\bar{c}} \{V(x(c)) - C(x(c), c) - (1 - \beta)\beta^{-1} - \bar{\pi}\}f(c)\, dc$$

$$- [2\beta - 1]\beta^{-1}\int_{c^-}^{\bar{c}} \pi(c)f(c)\, dc. \qquad (A3.10)$$

Now, integrating (by parts) the last integral on the right-side of (A3.10), one obtains

$$[2\beta - 1]\beta^{-1}\int_{c^-}^{\bar{c}} \pi(c)f(c)\, dc$$

$$= -\int_{c^-}^{\bar{c}} \pi'(c)H(c)f(c)\, dc + [2\beta - 1]\beta^{-1}\bar{\pi}F(\bar{c})$$

$$= \int_{c^-}^{\bar{c}} C_c(x(c), c)H(c)f(c)\, dc$$

$$+ [2\beta - 1]\beta^{-1}\bar{\pi}F(\bar{c}) \quad \text{(using (A3.4))}. \qquad (A3.11)$$

Substituting (A3.11) into (A3.10) yields the "transformed" objective function for [RP-C].

Index